THE THREE WORLDS OF BORIS PASTERNAK

The Gold of Troy
The Holy Fire
Fathers of The Western Church
Forever China
Schweitzer: Hero of Africa
Zero
The Terrorists
Mao Tse-Tung
The White Rajahs of Sarawak
The Holy Sword
The Splendour of Greece
Gershwin

The
Three Worlds
of
Boris Pasternak

by

ROBERT PAYNE

LONDON
ROBERT HALE LIMITED

71-01206

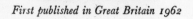

First published in Great Britain 1962

For
My Mother
and
Father

Printed in Great Britain by Richard Clay and Company Ltd.,
Bungay, Suffolk

Contents

Introduction

THE CREATIVE fire works mysteriously, and we shall never know why Elizabethan England produced such a volcanic display of poets, or why Florence under the Medicis produced so many artists, or Vienna under the Hapsburgs so many musicians. No one has ever been able to explain why Russia in the nineteenth century, under the tyrannical Tzars, produced a classic age of literature.

Neither the court nor the Tzars gave encouragement to literature, yet the giants arose—Pushkin, Lermontov, Gogol, Dostoevsky, Turgenev, Leskov, Tolstoy, Chekhov. They came in quick succession, stepping on each other's toes, like men in haste to proclaim their discoveries about the human soul. How great they were we are only beginning to realize in our own day; and we live under their shadow. The wave which was brought into being by Pushkin reached its greatest height in the seventies, and with Chekhov's death in 1904 it seemed to lose itself in the sands. It was as though the Russian genius had spent itself, as though the tide were falling back. One last wave threw up the figures of Alexander Blok and Boris Pasternak, and then it was all over.

This book is a sketch for a portrait of Pasternak, the last of the giants who had their roots in the nineteenth century. I have attempted to describe him under three aspects: as poet, as novelist, as political figure; all the more a political figure because he avoided political statements until the last years of his life. Inevitably the portrait is unfair to his contemporaries, for there was no space to do more than sketch in the background. Yet if in the following pages he often appears to be walking alone, there is some justice in it: he walked alone most of his life, with all the massed power of the Soviets against him.

I have tried to hold the balance between the poet and the prose writer fairly. His short stories are still too little known, and they are here discussed at considerable length. In the chapter on *Doctor Zhivago* I have dealt chiefly with the characters of Yury Zhivago and Larissa Guishar, and avoided the temptation to discuss their complicated adventures at length. Long commentaries have been written on James Joyce's *Ulysses*, and inevitably they will be written on *Doctor Zhivago*. It was no part of my purpose to add complexities to those that already exist.

Pasternak's poetry has been translated literally, with no attempt to produce rhymes and assonances. The selections have been designed to offer a brief anthology of the very best of his poems and the finest of his prose passages. Except for a few lines, *The Year Nineteen Five* has been translated into prose, because there is no better way to suggest the brisk and controlled movement of his free verse.

I owe a special debt of gratitude to Countess Alexandra Tolstoy, who kindly gave me her memories of the visits of the Pasternak family in Yasnaya Polyana, to Prince Alexis Scherbatow who carefully read through my manuscript and gave me the benefit of his immense erudition, and to Madame Olga Zhigalova, who knew the Pasternak family in Berlin and supplied me with details which I would not otherwise have known.

Above all there is a debt of which I have been conscious throughout the writing of this book: to the poetess Anna Akhmatova, who in Paris as far back as 1938 liked to talk about the man whom she called simply 'the poet', because it seemed to her that no other poet was worth talking about.

ONE

The Childhood of a Poet

WHEN Boris Pasternak was born, Moscow was still medieval. It was a city of ferocious contrasts—brilliantly coloured golden-domed churches, immense palaces, imposing streets, and always very close to them were wooden huts, dark alley-ways, rotting tenements, the smell of the black earth. The earth indeed was very close to Moscow, and her moods depended upon the seasons. It was not so much a city as a village vastly magnified, with the lord of the manor in-habiting the Kremlin, while his knights lived in palaces arranged haphazardly around him; and between the palaces were slums.

In those days Moscow was no longer the official capital of Russia: that honour belonged to St. Petersburg, designed largely by Italian architects on the banks of the Neva in the cold northern marshlands. St. Petersburg looked outward to the Baltic and the future; Moscow looked inward, into the heart of Russia and into the past, even the remote past. Almost, Moscow belonged to the forests, and those churches resem-bling brightly painted flowers and exotic vegetables hinted at the prevailing presence of the earth-gods who were worshipped until Christianity arrived in the tenth century. History lay lightly on St. Petersburg, but it lay heavy on Moscow. St. Petersburg was new; Moscow was old, wrinkled, faded, like an old dowager loaded with jewels.

Over the years the Muscovites had retained their Russian feeling; they had escaped the full impact of Western civiliza-tion. They wore the Russian blouse, heavy trousers and top boots, and were inclined to look down on the people of St. Petersburg who aped Western dress and Western manners. They spoke with broader vowels, and were more exuberant, more colourful, quick-witted and earthy than the men of the north. In that great sprawling city every day was a festival, and every street a fairground.

The Muscovites prided themselves on their tolerance; they regarded themselves as belonging to an old race which had seen empires rise and fall; and in their attitude toward the people of St. Petersburg they were like Romans complaining against the Milanese or the Florentines. They spoke of Moscow as 'the third Rome', the inheritor of Byzantium under the Caesars. Though the Tzar ruled from St. Petersburg, and all power reposed in him, no one ever regarded St. Petersburg as 'the third Rome'. The Muscovites regarded Moscow as the real capital, and they were content to wait patiently for the day when the Tzar would abandon his Italian city in the north.

In the Kremlin, where he was crowned and where he stayed on frequent visits from the capital, the Tzar dined off gold plate studded with emeralds, and in the palaces of the courtiers and merchant princes, who were beginning to exert their new-found power, unbelievable luxury ruled. Wealth was naked; and so was poverty. In all the world there was perhaps no city where there was so much abject poverty side by side with barbaric wealth and splendour.

Boris Pasternak was born in one of the poorer districts of Moscow, in a house that was drab and down-at-heels, on the edge of the slums. It was a large house, two stories high, once a palace, now divided up into apartments, with a great central courtyard. The apartment where he was born was built over the vaulted archway, and his first memories were of the coach-men flicking their whips as they wheeled boisterously into the yard below.

In the time of Peter the Great there had been a munitions factory in the street, supplying weapons and armour for all of Moscow, but those days had passed. It was still called Arsenal Street—Oruzheyny Pereulok—and there was about those large stone houses an air of faded gentility. Nearby were the meat markets and the slums of the Truba. There were many stables in the neighbourhood, and many horse jobbers, usually Tartars wearing colourful caftans. There was the smell of horse dung and horsemeat, and in summer the flies were everywhere.

It was a strange, wild vivid place, sweating with poverty, noisy, filled with throngs of people from all over Russia, shouting in half a dozen languages. Walking down this street you would come upon beggars and ragpickers and the sellers of caged canaries. A cabdriver would be beating up his mistress, and a drunken Tartar would be driving a cart with a dead horse slung over it on the way to the horsemeat factory. Years later Boris spoke of the procession of dead horses, 'bright blue with intelligent marble heads', which were always passing beneath the window. He remembered too the theological school on the other side of the road with the painted railings, and the young divinity students in their long black gowns playing wildly in the garden among the artificial mounds and lakes during their free hours. Of the apartment over the gateway he remembered only that it was small and there were many paintings and drawings on the walls, and he always wanted to run out and talk to the bearded coachmen and all the other strange people who thronged the street, but his nurse prevented him.

He was born on February 10, 1890. His father, Leonid Ossipovich Pasternak, had intended to be a doctor and studied medicine at Moscow University, but gave it up to devote himself to painting. He was twenty-eight, and still a struggling painter with very little achievement. He had fair hair and blue eyes.

Born in Odessa, he was a Jew, descended from a long line of Sephardic Jews who had settled in Salonica and Central Europe before coming to Russia towards the beginning of the eighteenth century. The name Pasternak means 'parsnip' in Russian.

Boris's mother, Rosalia Isidorovna Kaufmann, was born in Odessa, the daughter of a soda-water manufacturer of German origin, a man of considerable importance in the community. She too was Jewish. A talented pianist, she had been the student of Leschetizky, and she had enjoyed a brief period of fame as a protégée of Anton Rubinstein when she was in her teens, giving piano recitals in Moscow, St. Petersburg and Warsaw. A great musical future was prophesied for her, but ill health prevented her from living up to Anton Rubinstein's expectations. She was a twenty-year-old professor of music in the Conserva-

tory at Odessa when she met and married her husband in 1887.
After the marriage she abandoned her musical career and devoted herself to her husband and bringing up her family. She
was small and plump, with big brown eyes, which Boris
inherited.

Leonid Pasternak was lean, wiry, impulsive, given to flashes
of temperament, with fine manners and a taste for fine clothes,
and very real gifts as a painter. Rosalia was gentle, imperturb-
able, and suffered from a bad heart. They admirably comple-
mented one another. They always regarded Moscow as their
home, but in fact their roots were in Odessa, in those days a
cosmopolitan city rivalling Vienna in its elegance, crowded with
a flourishing community of Jewish intellectuals—doctors, law-
yers, musicians, artists of all kinds. Odessa was an eastern
Naples, wholly Oriental in flavour, a wonderful forcing ground
for young talents; and the restrictions on the Jews, which were
enforced in most of the other Russian cities, were notably absent
there. It was in Odessa, during the time of Bialyk and Tcher-
nokovsky, that modern Hebrew poetry took its rise. Isaac
Babel called it 'our God-fearing city, the star of our exile, the
involuntary well of our distress'.

Of those early years in the apartment over the gateway
Boris Pasternak remembered very little, for he was only three
when his parents moved to another part of the town. He remembered, of course, the view from the window, and he remembered being taken one damp autumn day through the
gardens of the theological seminary, and asking questions about
the strange characters who paraded through the street, and
being told not to ask questions about them because their behaviour was beyond the understanding of small boys. His nurse
sang him to sleep with a strange little song:

> Sleep well, my child, sleep well.
> When you are grown up,
> I will do no more painting,
> I will have others to do it for me.

The nurse was evidently celebrating the day when her master's
fortunes would improve.

The turning point in Leonid Pasternak's fortunes came in 1892, when he was invited to contribute to a de luxe edition of *War and Peace*. The other painters who were invited were Repin, Verestchaguin and Kivschenko, all of them famous, and the first two were in fact the most famous and successful Russian painters of the time. The invitation came in the autumn of the year, and soon the artist was discussing his charcoal drawings with Tolstoy, who was spending the winter in Moscow. He made a good impression on Tolstoy, and drew the first of the long series of drawings of Tolstoy which he continued to draw until the novelist's death. For the next twenty years the Pasternaks were to remain intimate friends of the Tolstoys.

Henceforth Leonid Pasternak was no longer a struggling young painter. Commissions poured in on him. He had the cultivated air of a man of the world, talked easily and well, and showed himself to advantage in Moscow society. And when in the following year the position of director of the Moscow School of Painting, Sculpture and Architecture fell vacant, he obtained the post on the recommendation of Repin. The school was under the patronage of the Grand Duke Sergey Alexandrovich, and the president of the school was Prince Lvov. Leonid Pasternak's fortunes were changing rapidly, for he now possessed a secure annual income besides the money he made from portraits and book illustrations and from giving private lessons in drawing to fashionable young ladies in his studio on the sixth floor. Instead of an apartment over a gateway, he was now installed in one of the palatial wings of the school in a fashionable neighbourhood of Moscow. There he remained, with his growing family, for the next sixteen or seventeen years.

The School of Painting was a large Italianate house, not unlike many others built in the early years of Catherine the Great, with imposing columns, vast curving stairways, and conference rooms lit by chandeliers. The wings, which were added later, were not quite so imposing, but the rooms were large and comfortably furnished, and the proportions were in remarkably good taste. There were large windows looking out over the courtyard, and more looking out over the street. No rough burly cabdrivers penetrated the courtyard. Instead there was a continual stream of fashionable coaches driven by elegant young coachmen who dressed like young noblemen and wore cockades in their hats. More than half of the pupils were girls, many of them the daughters of the nobility and the merchant princes. Leonid Pasternak was moving into a position of power and affluence.

The school stood on one of the corners of the Myasnitskaya, 'the Street of the Butchers', one of those immensely long, tree-lined avenues radiating out from the centre of the city. At one end of the street was the great Lubyanskaya Square; at the other end was the Kazan railway station. About halfway between the square and the railway station was the school, and opposite the school was the Central Post Office and the Telegraph Office. Anyone living at the school was therefore in an admirable position to watch the great processions which sometimes moved down the long avenue.

Young Boris, aged four, stood on the balcony and watched the funeral procession of Alexander III which left the Kremlin and wound through the streets of Moscow to the railway station. Black crape hung over the walls of the school and over all the houses of the street. Everything was drenched in darkness. Black horses, black-clothed priests, black plumes on the horses, black mourning bands on the soldiers who walked at a slow funeral pace in endless columns along the street. A Tzar's funeral in Russia was an occasion for splendour. Priests robed in the finest damasks and embroidered silks, officers wearing the slashed and fur-trimmed costumes of six-teenth-century boyars, kings and princes in a variety of gold-laced uniforms followed the coffin, while the two hundred churches of Moscow pealed a slow lament. Two years later, in 1895, there came another procession moving in the reverse direction. The new Tzar, Nicholas II, came from St. Peters-burg to be crowned in the Cathedral of the Assumption in the Kremlin. It was a very bright day, and the sun glittered on the jewelled panoply which hurried below the small balcony and vanished into the distance. This time the church bells rang joyfully, and they were still ringing late at night.

Such processions are never forgotten, but Boris remembered still more vividly an event which occurred in the same year

that saw the funeral procession of Alexander III. He remembered waking up at night and hearing music. For some
reason the music made him frightened and he burst out crying.
He was sleeping behind a curtain, and his mother came to
him quickly. When the curtain parted he had a glimpse of a
room which seemed like paradise. There were candles everywhere, and the room was filled with smoke, and the necks and
shoulders of women were gleaming. He realized it was a
musical concert, and all these elegant guests had been invited
to attend. In particular one of these guests attracted his
attention, a tall, ruddy-faced man with an immense grey
beard. It was Count Leo Tolstoy, who ever afterward seemed
to haunt the house with his beneficent presence.

Leonid Pasternak was moving in exalted circles. He was
invited everywhere. He attended receptions given by the
princely families, and indefatigably sketched their daughters—
he possessed an extraordinary skill in catching a likeness in a
few seconds. One of his closest friends was the portrait painter
Valentin Serov, and they sometimes went to the receptions
together and made sketches of the same people and compared them. His wife rarely attended these functions. She
was usually busy at home making up accounts, answering
correspondence, arranging for exhibitions of her husband's
work, and busying herself with his contracts for book illustrations. She was one of those serious, sensible women who know
exactly how to manage affairs, and she ran the house like
clockwork. She rarely played the piano, except for her own
family. Leonid was easily depressed; Rosalia was always
smiling.

The years passed, and Boris grew up to the sound of music,
with the smell of turpentine in his nostrils. Sometimes when
his father was painting, he would be called in to amuse the
sitters. He was a grave eager boy, easily hurt, fastidious, who
liked to wear clean clothes and who was already passionately
fond of music. His father had studied painting in Munich and
spoke German well, and Boris picked up German as rapidly
as he picked up Russian. Occasionally Tolstoy would drop
into the house, and Boris watched him with open-mouthed
adoration.

Toward the end of 1898, when Tolstoy was coming to the end of his long novel *Resurrection*, it occurred to him that Leonid was the best man to do the illustrations. This time there was to be no sharing of the illustrations: all of them were to be done by the same artist. Invited to Yasnaya Polyana, Tolstoy's country estate near Tula, Leonid brought his whole family with him. There were endless discussions. Tolstoy was continually making changes in the story, and sometimes entire chapters were cut out of the novel, with the result that some of Leonid's drawings were abandoned. The artist had the freedom of the house. When he was not sketching the peasants in the fields, he would sketch Tolstoy at his desk, chopping wood, mowing hay, walking in the forest, or taking his afternoon nap. Photographs of Tolstoy taken at this time are misleading; he looks gaunt, reserved, ill at ease, perhaps because he detested photographers. Leonid's drawings and occasional paintings restore the balance. They suggest a ruddy-faced giant with a quick intense body, still supple at the age of seventy. And when the Pasternaks returned to Moscow, it was Rosalia who went out into the streets and found the peasant women who served as models for her husband's illustrations. She would hold their hands if they were nervous, and mother them, and see that they were fed. Soon the studio was crowded with peasants of all kinds, all seeking to be models.

For almost a year these illustrations were the consuming passion of Leonid's life, but it was Rosalia who had to see the printers and lithographers and publishers, and run to the post office with the proofs to be sent to Tolstoy. Since the studio was sacred territory, all the packaging and letter writing was done in the kitchen.

Sometimes, when there was an unusually urgent parcel to be delivered, the services of the railway guards would be used. This was not difficult, since one of Boris's uncles was a high official on the railways. Then it would happen that an amused Boris would find a guard in full uniform standing outside the kitchen, exactly as though he were standing beside a train, waiting for it to depart. Meanwhile there would be joiner's glue boiling on the stove, and on the littered table the illustrations for *Resurrection* were being hastily glued to sheets of cardboard, which were then rolled up, wrapped in paper, and sealed with sealing wax. All through that year there was never-ending excitement over the illustrations.

One day in July 1898, a few months before Leonid was over-whelmed with the commission to illustrate *Resurrection* and vanished from his normal world, he did a pencil sketch of his eldest son—another son, Alexander, was born in 1893—as he sat over the drawing-room table. It is one of the best of his sketches. The boy is engrossed in sketching, leaning forward a little, one bare foot curled around the other. He wears the full Russian blouse, and his hair is cut short, as it always is with Russian children. Boris still has baby fat on his cheeks, but as he writes he is wholly absorbed in the world he is creating. Never again did the father capture that look of intense absorption. He made many portraits of his son, but in most of them there is a curious solemnity and stiffness. In his father's eyes, quite early, the boy assumed the aspect of a stranger. Leonid was puzzled by the son who had inherited none of his own gifts, who was always reading and scribbling, and who spoke even in those days in a painfully slow, deliberate and musical voice. But though Boris often puzzled his parents, he was intensely affectionate, and inherited from his parents the music and colour which appears in his poetry.

By 1900 Leonid could afford to take his family on long summer holidays in the south. That summer he took the whole family to Odessa. One morning, very early, they climbed on to the train at the Kursk station in Moscow, and they were waiting for the train to depart when Boris saw a small man in a black Tyrolean cape hurrying along the platform, accom-panied by a woman who was his mother or an elder sister. The small man stopped to talk with Leonid, and though they spoke in German, a language which Boris usually understood, he had difficulty in understanding what the man was saying. The man vanished, but appeared later to ask whether the train would stop at the wayside station of Kozlovka, whence it was only a short drive to Tolstoy's estate at Yasnaya Polyana. He was agitated, but Leonid was able to calm him, and at Kozlovka the train came to an abrupt halt and the strange

German got out and entered a waiting carriage for the journey to Yasnaya Polyana.

Boris remembered the scene vividly and described it at length in his autobiography, *The Safe Conduct*. He remembered it moment by moment, in all its details. He wrote:

> Then with relief the cloud-piled sky tore itself from the whirlwind of singing sand, and skirting the grove of birch trees an empty carriage and pair, flung forward as though dancing the *russkaya*, fluttered to the feet of the passengers who had just alighted. The silence of the halt, so curiously indifferent to us, absorbed the momentary excitement like a gunshot. It was not for us to stay here. They waved their handkerchiefs in farewell, and we waved back. I could see the coachman with his long red sleeves helping them up, handing the lady a rug, half rising in his seat to adjust his belt, and gathering the long skirts of his peasant coat. In a moment they would be off. But the curve in the railway was already catching up with us, and the wayside station turned slowly like a page which has been read, and vanished from sight. Face and incident were forgotten, presumably forever.

In spite of the rococo beginning, it is an interesting passage, admirably conveying the child's excitement, his sense of wonder at the strange man who spoke Geman with a pronounced accent, his regret when they disappeared from view and the train went on in the direction of Odessa. The stranger was the Austrian poet, Rainer Maria Rilke. Boris was so impressed by the encounter that he devoted the opening pages of his autobiography to his first meeting with a great poet, and he was inclined to attach extraordinary importance to it.

Curiously, Boris's memory of the meeting is largely imaginary, and he never saw Rilke step down on to the platform of a wayside station and climb into a carriage driven by a coachman 'with long red sleeves', either then or at any other time. He did not, of course, invent the story. He merely confused two separate incidents, as children do, and long afterward he believed they had actually happened simultaneously.

Both Leonid and Rilke have left records of that journey.

Leonid writes briefly, Rilke at considerable length in a letter to a friend. Leonid, in some brief extracts from an unfinished autobiography attached to a sumptuous edition of reproductions of his paintings, remembered distinctly that there were three people—Rilke, Lou Andreas-Salome and her husband, a doctor. Rilke remembered the whole series of events, writing them down a few hours later. Writing from Tula on May 20, 1900, to his close friend Sophie Schill, Rilke speaks of meeting Professor Pasternak on the train and discussing whether it would be possible to see Tolstoy. The professor was not over helpful; all he could suggest was that there was a certain Mr. Boulanger on the train who would know exactly where Tolstoy could be found. Rilke followed the advice of Mr. Boulanger, stopped off at Tula, where he received no answer to the telegram he had sent to Yasnaya Polyana, and it was some days before he was able to visit the estate. Tolstoy was not too pleased with the visit, and Rilke has drawn a faintly acid portrait of the great man, whom he had met once before in Leonid's studio in Moscow. According to Rilke, Tolstoy proposed a walk through the park, gathered some flowers, held them up to his nostrils in his cupped hands, and then threw them away. 'Sometimes in the wind the figure of the Count grew; his great beard fluttered, but the grave face, marked by solitude, remained quiet, as though untouched by the storm.'[1] After the walk, Rilke and his companions returned to Kozlovka on foot. They had spent perhaps no more than an hour with Tolstoy.

Boris remembered meeting Rilke, and he remembered the carriage waiting at Kozlovka, presided over by a coachman 'with long red sleeves', from another visit. He had fused together two entirely different events; fused them so completely and appropriately that he always believed he had seen Rilke on his way to Yasnaya Polyana, and his memory always gave him pleasure. In much the same way he fused together in his prose and poetry the most diverse and unlikely objects. In him there was a constant and absorbing preoccupation to

---

[1] *Letters of Rainer Maria Rilke: 1892–1910*, translated by Jane Bannard Greene and M. D. Herter Norton. New York: W. W. Norton and Company, 1945, p. 42.

relate entirely different objects to one another, so that he was able to say that the evening was like the blue bag of washed linen which a patient takes home from the hospital, or he would say, as though it were the most natural thing in the world, that 'the sunset was drenched in pomegranate juice'. A vast amount of his later poetry, and many of his most dazzling ideas, have their origin in the deliberate confusion of concepts which are totally different from one another.

Boris had met Rilke, and soon he was to meet Scriabin, the composer, who had an even greater influence on him. In the spring of 1903 Leonid rented a house at Obolenskoye, a small village near the town of Malo-Yaroslavets, about seventy-five miles south-west of Moscow. It was a small country *dacha* set among woods and streams, very quiet and peaceful. The family, laden down with bedding and kitchen utensils, arrived early in the morning, and Boris immediately slipped away into the woods. He was completely enchanted by the woods and by the sound of someone playing music in a house not far away. It was Scriabin composing his Third Symphony (*Poème Divin*), and Boris had never heard any music like it. He was spellbound by its freshness, by a quality of ecstasy which was not very far from frenzy. It was fresh, light, incredibly complex, and wholly original. Sometimes it was mischievous and playfully elemental, and for some reason it reminded him in later years of the free flight of a fallen angel. Intoxicated by the music, he ran home and insisted on being taken to see the composer.

Some time later Scriabin went completely mad, but at this time he was still in full command of his faculties and had not yet identified himself with God. He was a slight, delicate, wispy man, with a Vandyke beard, a high forehead, small brown eyes, and a nervous manner which sometimes gave place to a kind of dictatorial fervour. He could be terrible in his rages. Sometimes he gave the impression of two completely different people living side by side: a gentle poet, and a screaming monomaniac who believed that all the people of the world would come to worship him. 'The world seeks after God,' he wrote in his diary. 'I seek after myself. The world is impelled toward God, I am impelled toward myself,

I am the world, I am the search for God, because I am only that which I seek.' Believing he was the Messiah, he sometimes preached on a boat anchored on Lake Geneva.

In the summer of 1903 Scriabin was still predominantly the virtuoso rejoicing in his powers as a pianist and composer, with the dangerous mystical period lying in front of him. He was thirty-one, brimming with energy. Boris, aged thirteen, fell hopelessly in love with him, followed him on long walks through the woods, and listened with wild-eyed excitement to the arguments between his father and this new-found friend who radiated enthusiasm. Scriabin became 'my god and my idol'. All through the early summer the composer worked on his Third Symphony, and Boris spent every morning in a delirium of joy listening to the music as it poured off the piano—that symphony which was 'like a city falling before artillery fire, and forever rising again out of its own ruins'. What surprised Boris above everything else was that after a morning spent in hammering the keyboard and improvising music which was like a continual crescendo of thunder and lightning, Scriabin would rise from the piano completely refreshed, so calm 'that he was like God resting from his labours on the seventh day'.

It was an exciting summer. There was Scriabin's music, and Scriabin wandering through the woods with his strange skipping walk, and a student drowned in the river, and a house caught fire, causing Leonid's hair to turn grey, for he was returning from Malo-Yaroslavets when he saw the red glare on the clouds and thought the house was his own. One day in the autumn, shortly before the family was due to return to Moscow, Leonid was making studies for a painting of village girls rounding up horses and driving them to the water meadows in the sunset. Boris rode out with his father, his horse threw him when he was jumping over a stream, and his leg was broken. For weeks the leg was kept in a plaster cast. It did not set properly, and when the plaster cast was removed, it was discovered that one leg was shorter than the other, and so it remained. In later years Pasternak commented wryly that the broken leg preserved him from participating in three wars.

While he was pinned down to the bed with a plaster cast,

Boris made the decision which ruled the next six years of his life. At all costs he would become a musician, following in the path of Scriabin. His family encouraged him and paid for his tuition, first under Yuri Engel, who was a close friend of Scriabin's, and then under Reinhold Glière, later to become a famous composer. Boris went to school, paid the proper tribute to mathematics, Greek and Latin, and thought only of composing. He had no fluency in sight reading, and never had the makings of a concert pianist, but he was a gifted composer. When Scriabin returned to Moscow in January 1909, after an absence of nearly five years spent in Switzerland, France, Belgium and the United States, Boris went to see him.

It was one of those cold wintry days with the rooks cawing in the trees, and all Moscow seemed to be drowning in the rain. But in Scriabin's studio everything was warm, comfortable, alive with electric excitement. Boris brought his own compositions, played for the master, and was greeted with a bravura performance. In his autobiography, *The Safe Conduct*, he relates the story of that interview:

He was pleased by my composition, and I hastened to finish playing. At once he began to assure me it would be absurd to speak of my musicianly gifts when he was confronted with so much more, and went on to say that I was destined to add my word to music. Remembering phrases which had flashed by, he sat down at the piano and repeated one which particularly attracted him. The harmony was complicated, and I hardly expected him to reproduce it accurately, but an unexpected thing happened—he repeated it in another key, and the flaws which had tormented me all these years splashed from under his fingers as though they were his own.

And then, preferring the eloquence of facts rather than the unreliability of guesses, I trembled and fell to thinking along two different lines of thought. If he said: 'Borya, neither do I have a sense of absolute pitch', then all would be well. That would mean I was not wrapping myself around music, but music had claimed me for its own. But if he answered by talking about Wagner and Tchaikovsky and

piano tuners and so on, then . . . I was already approaching
this nerve-racking subject when I was interrupted in the
middle of a word and forced to swallow his reply. He was
saying: 'What is this about absolute pitch? After everything I have been telling you? What about Wagner and
Tchaikovsky? And there are hundreds of tuners who have
it, too!'

It was an extraordinary moment—the young and unknown
composer putting the older man on trial, and gambling his
whole life on the outcome. Scriabin was found wanting. He
had made the inevitable, the vulgar, the intolerable reply to
the simple question whether one could be a great composer
while lacking a sense of absolute pitch, and in that moment
Boris quite irrationally decided to abandon music. The idol
had feet of clay, but still wore his crown. Boris continued to
respect the composer, but could no longer possess an absolute
veneration for him. For a few more minutes they continued
talking. Scriabin asked what he was studying at the University. Boris answered that he had chosen to enter the law school,
'because it is easy', and Scriabin gently suggested that this
was a mistake: he should study philosophy. The next day
Boris entered the philosophy school at the University.

It was evening when Boris left Scriabin's studio, and the
street lamps were lit in the street outside. 'As I bade him
good-bye, I did not know how to thank him. Something welled
up within me. It tore me and strove to be free. Something
wept, something exulted.'

Just over three years before, in December 1905, there had
been another moment when 'something wept, something exulted'. It happened during the December uprising in Moscow
when a Cossack whip cut across his quilted coat.

TWO

The Year Nineteen Five

In the year 1905, when Pasternak was fourteen, Russia began to break apart. It was not a slow breaking. Quite suddenly, as the result of centuries of mismanagement, the entire fabric of the Russian state began to crumble.

The year opened unpromisingly. On January 9 the priest Gapon led a vast procession of about 200,000 people through the streets of St. Petersburg to present a petition to the Tzar. The priest wore his flowing black robes, and the people carried banners and portraits of the Tzar and the royal family; they sang religious hymns and seemed to be caught up in a religious ecstasy. It was an intensely cold day, with blue skies and crisp snow on the ground. When the procession reached the great square outside the Winter Palace, the Cossacks opened fire. When the smoke cleared there were 150 dead and more than 300 wounded; and the snow outside the Winter Palace turned red.

This was the beginning, and from that moment there could be no retreat. War was declared between the people and the autocracy—a savage and unremitting war, which could have only one ending. Gapon, who later became a double agent, proclaimed that there was only one way to destroy Tzarism. 'Bombs and dynamite, terror by individuals and by the masses are needed now.' Less than a month later, on February 4, a young student called Ivan Kaliayev threw a bomb at the Grand Duke Sergey Alexandrovich, the uncle of the Tzar, as he was leaving his palace in the Kremlin. The Grand Duke was killed instantly. The assassin quietly surrendered, and was hanged.

At fourteen Pasternak was an acutely sensitive youth, dark-faced, moody, in love with music and painting, almost deliriously happy in his home life, with very little knowledge of the world outside, except that which he derived from the long daily journey to school and back again. His school was in the Povarskaya, on the other side of Moscow, in the run-down Arbat district, a network of evil-smelling alley-ways, with its thieves' dens and wooden houses rotting at the foundations. He hated the tram journey which took him to school. He hated limping through the snow during the long winter. Over all this region of Moscow fear reigned—the damp squalid fear of the poor, the disinherited, the eternal drunkards. At night, fires were lit at the crossroads and the smoke drifted over the city and the smell of burning wet wood was everywhere. Pasternak hated the place so much that he deliberately placed Doctor Zhivago's death in a tram not more than a stone's throw away from the school.

But if he disliked school—and he was never a brilliant student—he rejoiced in his family. The hateful journeys to school were forgotten in the warmth engendered by his parents at home: the piano open all day, canvases everywhere, famous visitors continually coming to pose, his father wearing a painter's smock which was like a Jacob's cloak of all colours, and always those bursts of sudden laughter which went running through the house like the running flames on the oil-soaked threads of the candles in Orthodox churches. Leonid Pasternak was an excellent mimic and told stories well. There were feasts and charades. There were birthdays and saints' days to be celebrated. Boris was already composing music, in helpless awe of Scriabin, whose occasional visits were accompanied by a good deal of noise and excitement; and sometimes, unable to bear the excitement, Boris fled to a dark corner to avoid seeing the man who was more like a god than anyone else he knew.

He had just returned to school after the holidays when he heard of the massacre outside the Winter Palace in St. Petersburg. All of Moscow was thrown into a frenzy of rumour and conjecture. The Tzar had abdicated! The border provinces were rising! The Japanese had landed on the soil of European Russia! Most of these rumours proved to be untrue, but there were in fact risings in the border provinces, and for the first time revolutionary speeches were being made openly, under the eyes of the police. All of Russia was in ferment. Though there were no armed insurrectionary outbreaks in Moscow—these

were to come later in the year—there were ill-organized out-
breaks in most of the major cities of Russia including St.
Petersburg, where the workmen held out for days on Vasilievsky
Island. The Tzar announced a conciliatory policy, but the
Tzardom was doomed.

Boris was at exactly the right age to feel the full force of the
tragedy. His impressionable mind recorded all the subtle
alterations of mood which swept over Moscow. It was a year of
destiny to be remembered always, and he described the events
of that year in one of the early chapters of *Doctor Zhivago* and
in the longest of his poems, which he called simply *The Year
Nineteen Five*. The poem has six parts. The first, called 'The
Fathers', describes the forerunners, those ardent revolutionaries who fought against the autocracy in the eighties of the last
century. The poet summons up the images of their defeat—the
brilliant Sophie Perovskaya hanged for attempting to murder
the Tzar Alexander II, the incredible Sergey Nechayev, who
proclaimed the total destruction of the state and showed how it
could be brought about, the insanely daring Stepan Khalturin
who lit the fuse to a packet of dynamite in the Winter Palace
and then calmly walked out of the building, and many more.

> Dostoevsky was among them,
> And so were those saintly women
> Who lived in seclusion,
> Never expecting
> That every search party
> Sent into their houses
> Would discover
> Relics for our museums,
> And went to their executions
> Never knowing
> That Nechayev, the underground man,
> Had hidden their beauty in the earth,
> Concealing it from
> The age of enemies and friends.

'The Fathers' is a quick impressionistic summary of those
times, when the serfs, though free, walked in a no man's land,
and there were revolutionaries everywhere, and Russia trembled

before the inevitable explosion. This first part ends characteristically with the image, which he used again in *Doctor
Zhivago*, of a man crashing into a blind lamp-post at night.

Like all Pasternak's poems, *The Year Nineteen Five* is quite
extraordinarily close-knit, charged with energy, intensely
coloured. He liked to speak of verses 'which bite the page', and
these verses have teeth in them. Long sweeping lines are followed by brisk staccato ones. He permits himself the widest
freedom and a dazzling display of imagery, employing rhyme
and assonance as he pleases, jumping from one event to another,
one city to another, one mood to another, as the spirit moves
him. All attempts to translate the poem into English have
failed, and it seems better to translate it into prose. Here is the
second movement, called 'Childhood', in which he describes
some of his own experiences during the early part of that tragic
year and simultaneously paints an unforgettable picture of
'Bloody Sunday' in St. Petersburg:

> *I was fourteen years old. The school of applied art was still a
> school of sculpture. In the wing where the workers' faculty now
> assembles, there was my father's studio, upstairs, a quarter of a mile
> away, where the dust of ages veiled Diana and the canvases—our door.
> Flagstones on the floor, and on the flagstones slush.*

> *These were the deep forests of winter. The kingdom of the lamps
> reigned in December. Port Arthur had already surrendered, but the
> cruisers still steamed across the ocean: armies were dispatched,
> squadrons were waited for, and the twilight gazed on the old post
> office, paints, palettes, and professors.*

> *So many portraits, so many faces! There an idiot, here a block-
> head! In one a flame burns, the other's a nincompoop. No room
> in the classroom for an apple to fall—warm as a hothouse. The bells
> of Sts. Florus and Laurus[1] blend with the shuffling feet.*

> *A tremendous noise behind the wall: the surf pouring in relentlessly,
> and the lake of the room was absolutely still. The streets alive with
> gas, and the doorbell rings. Voices coming closer. Scriabin! Where
> shall I hide from the footsteps of my god?*

[1] The church adjoined the School of Painting on the Myasnitskaya.

Holidays looming closer, quarterly reports, end of the half year. The piano lay open, showing its shining sinews throughout the day. Compose music from the hour of dawn! The days wandering away, and Christmas is dying. We give so much to our Christmas trees. If only there was a little return!

Night. Petersburg. The air swelling dark with snowflakes under needling footsteps. No streets are forbidden to those in heavy coats, to those in sheepskins. The moon shrinks with cold to the size of a silver coin. The Narva district stirs. The crowd roars: Gapon!

Ringing voices in the hall, and the airless heat. The trees watched five thousand pass. The snow drifts from the street into hallways, clings to the stairs. Here is the new maternity, and in the unpainted vaulted womb there pulses against the walls a strange unlovely lump— the age we live in.

Glorious dawn, the clouds like berries. We hear the creaking of passageways, the smoky steam of slop water. They hurry away and go from the hall to the gate under the sacred banners, and from the gates out into the cold, into the empty spaces, on fire with winter.

Eight roaring waves, and then the ninth—majestic as spaces. Hats washed off their heads. O Lord, save Thy people. A bridge and a ditch to the left. To the right the cemetery gates. Behind lies a forest: the telegraph wires are in front. On Kamenny Island the pavement stands on stilts, gaping from kiosks and pediments. Behind the procession swings the whip which breaks through the blocks of crossroads and thickening streets.

The demonstrators have reached the park, are marching over Trinity Bridge. Eight salvoes from the Neva, and then a ninth— weary like glory. Then—(To right and left, cavalry riding up at a trot.) Then—(The spaces thunder forth: Vengeance against the massacrers!) The oaths of loyalty sworn to the dynasty are broken at the joints.

The pavements are full of people running. Dusk deepens. Day will not rise again. The roar of the cannonade is answered by rifle fire from barricades. I am fourteen years old. In a month I will be fifteen. Those days are like a diary: you find something to read, opening at any page.

*We played with snowballs—caught them spinning out of the sky:
flakes of rumour, pieces of conversation. This is the landslide of
kingdoms, the drunken weaving of snow. There, in the courtyard of
the Gymnasium at the corner of the Povarskaya in January.*

*Storm of snow day after day. Those in the party have the look of
eagles: they are already grown-up. We are rude to the Greek
professor, and no one punishes us. We push our desks to the wall, play
at parliament during class, and dream of all the illegal happenings in
Gruzin.*

*For three days running the snow falls: at dusk it is still falling.
During the night it clears. The morning brings the thunderous news
from the Kremlin. The patron of the art school, Grand Duke Sergey
Alexandrovich, killed! In those early days of January I fell in love
with the storm.*

So Pasternak wrote twenty years after the event, weaving
Moscow and St. Petersburg together as though they were a
single city, seeing himself in the school playground as vividly as
he saw the march of the petitioners led by Gapon, who was
later murdered by the same revolutionary who helped him to
escape across the frontier. It was a time of incredible violence.
There were uprisings in Finland, Poland and the Ukraine. In
May there was the crushing naval defeat at Tsushima; within
a month the sailors on the battleship *Prince Potyomkin* rose in
rebellion.

The third movement of *The Year Nineteen Five*, called 'Peasants
and Factory Workers', describes the insurrection in the Polish
town of Lodz. It is the least successful of the six movements,
very short and perfunctory, written in a mood of revolutionary
resignation. The army smashes the revolt. 'But with every turn
of the gun wheels, one of these slaves fell, and with every cavalry
charge, the prestige of the autocracy went down.'

Though Pasternak showed very little poetic understanding of
the Polish uprisings, he was in his element when depicting the
mutiny on the *Prince Potyomkin*. He begins in the heroic mood
with a classic salutation to the sea:

*All palls. Only you have no chance. The days pass, the years are
endless. Washed in a welter of years and ages, in the white rage of*

waves, in the white trance of acacias, perhaps, O Sea, it is you who reduce everything to zero.

Throned on a mountain of nets, you shout to the skies, gay as the playful springtime, weaving a fugitive lock of hair around a sailor's brow, caressing the prows of ships, while children invite you to be their guest. But with what strange thunder you shout when the distant horizons summon you home!

Pasternak serves notice that he will describe the naval mutiny as though it were an episode in Homer. The sailors shoot the officers and throw some of them into the sea after an issue of rations running with maggots, then they hoist the red flag and sail for Odessa to go to the assistance of the strikers. The story is familiar from Eisenstein's film, *The Battleship Potyomkin*. It is a story of violence erupting so suddenly that both the officers and the sailors were taken unawares. Pasternak's verse becomes abrupt and soaring; it narrows on a particular incident, and takes flight over the entire Black Sea. It is the poetry of a man who has never been on a warship, and is no more concerned to provide an accurate minute-by-minute account of the mutiny than Homer was concerned to write a military history of the Trojan War. His hero, Afanasi Matushenko, is described in heroic proportions:

The sailors' hearts throbbed with fear, and one who could bear it no longer, shouted: 'Brothers, what are we up to?' Then, shaking his locks: 'Let's kill them, brothers! They're rotten! Long live liberty!' Out of the gun turrets the men leaped for the deck.

And the mutiny winged with rustling sound from the mizzen to the bridge, describing an arc of fire in the hovering wind. 'We've nothing to run from! Put an end to them! They're ours!' Trrraaak . . . Trrraaak . . . Trrraaak. . . . Like a paintbrush striking at the target, they picked off the enemy at random.

Trrrraaak . . . Trrrraaak . . . Trrrraaak . . . The bullets scattered along the deck, and from the deck came Trrrraaak . . . Trrrraaak . . . Trrrraaak . . . On the waves, on the men swimming below. 'Is that fellow still on the ship?' Volleys into the waves, into the air. Aha, so your grievances made you wild, eh? Volleys, volleys! And they lifted him by the feet and threw him overboard, for the march to Port Arthur.

In the roar of the engine room still the engineers knew nothing at all about the events on the quarter-deck. Then the shadow of a giant came marching over the gratings over the furnace: and Matushenko roared down into the infernal regions: 'Stepan, they're on the run!'

The chief engineer clambered up, embraced and laughed: 'We'll do without those nannies, eh?' 'They're under guard, and the rest we've shot, or they're feeding the fishes! What about it, Stepan? How about the junior engineer?' 'He's one of ours!' 'Good. Send him up to me, on the bridge.'

So the day ended, and at sunset smoke curtained the warship, as a sailor boomed through a megaphone to the men below: 'Weigh anchor!' The voice grew still in the clouds. Then the Prince Potyomkin *sailed for Odessa, forging a furrow of doom: against the sharp cliffs she shone like a rust-speckled flame.*

There Pasternak ends his brief fragment of an unfinished epic, omitting the subsequent adventures of the mutineers who finally sailed to Constanza on the Roumanian coast and were interned.[1] It is not among his best poems, but it is one of the most revealing. We see him occupied with violent action, capable of sustaining a violent mood, but completely incapable of suggesting even for a moment the concerted action of many men fighting. There is Matushenko, larger than life, larger than the boiler room, larger than the *Prince Potyomkin*. He not only dominates the scene, but the scene is in fact seen through his eyes, and he carries the full weight of the event. In much the same way Pasternak will describe the fighting in the Civil War in *Doctor Zhivago*, seeing all things through the calm eyes of the tall, red-bearded doctor.

The description of violent action is almost always beyond the scope of the lyric poet. He is more concerned with moods, with sudden leaping evocations of spiritual atmospheres. Pasternak's failures in describing the mutiny at sea can be compared with

[1] Matushenko, though the leader of the rebellion, was later offered a pardon. On his return he was arrested at the Austro-Russian frontier post, and hanged.

Gerard Manley Hopkins' failure to describe the shipwreck in
'The Wreck of the Deutschland':

> They fought with God's cold—
> And they could not and fell to the deck
> (Crushed them) or water (and drowned them) or rolled
> With the sea-romp over the wreck.
> Night roared, with the heart-break hearing a heart-broke
> rabble;
> The woman's wailing, the crying of child without
> check. . . .

In both poets the very intensity of the emotion destroys and
inhibits the capacity to relate the scene in its full context. The
individuals vanish; causality vanishes; and the poets see, not
historical events, but events *sub specie aeternitatis*. But since
events can never be seen or interpreted for any prolonged period
of time against an eternal panorama, both poets see fitfully, in
sudden blinding glimpses, with a kind of jagged vision which
sometimes suggests a man looking at a landscape in a snowstorm.
Characteristically, Pasternak concludes the fragment with the
warship sailing into the distance, becoming no more than an
orange-coloured speck.

With the two remaining movements of *The Year Nineteen Five*
Pasternak returned to Moscow, where he was at home, describing events he had watched with his own eyes—a student's
funeral as it wound through the grief-laden streets to the cemetery in the slums, and the December uprisings in Moscow, which
were put down with ferocious cruelty by soldiers of the Semyonovsky regiment.

Pasternak's description of the funeral of the student Nikolay
Baumann, killed by an agent of the secret police on October 18,
1905, takes the form of a slow lament. In silence the procession
follows the coffin. Once a woman screamed, but the silence only
grew deeper. It was bitterly cold, with the snow shrouding the
statue of Lomonosov in the University courtyard, where 'the
frost breathed blood'. The body of the young student is carried
to the Vagankov cemetery, where

> In the grass of a graveyard
> The stars
> Took up their habitation,

And the heavens slept,
Plunged
In a silver forest of chrysanthemums.

It is Pasternak writing at his most gentle, at his most lyrical. Violence returns in the final movement, called 'Moscow in December'.

That year there were two uprisings in Moscow. The first occurred in October, following the Tzar's October Manifesto promising the convocation of the Duma. It was a confused outbreak: the mobs came out of the slums and encouraged by the police pillaged the University and the schools, destroying everything they could lay their hands on. Even the School of Painting on the Myasnitskaya, where the Pasternaks were living, was threatened; and orders were given to have the fire hoses ready, to drench the looters when they came. Nearly all the advantages were in the hands of the police and the army, for the revolutionaries quarrelled hopelessly among themselves. The railway workers came out on strike. When a vast procession formed at the Tver Gate and began to march across the whole length of Moscow, the dragoons cut it to pieces. Young Boris ran out to watch the procession, and was bowled over by a Cossack who struck him across the shoulder and left him sprawling in the snow. He was not seriously hurt, but he never forgot the blow.

A more serious uprising occurred in December. For more than a week Moscow was in a state of armed insurrection, with hundreds of barricades straddled across the streets. The troops resorted to artillery fire. Houses sheltering the armed revolutionaries were shelled and set on fire.

The strongest and most determined revolutionaries were to be found among the railway workers of the Moscow–Kazan line, and these received exemplary punishment. Two officers of the Semyonovsky Guards Regiment were given a free hand to punish the railwaymen. Their instructions were 'to take no prisoners and act mercilessly'. Their names were Mein and Riemann; they were of German extraction; and they took a savage delight in bayoneting, shooting or hanging every railwayman they were able to capture. All along the track of the Moscow–Kazan line were the dead bodies of railwaymen

c

hanging from the telegraph poles. And when they had mopped
up these railwaymen, the two officers turned their attention to
the men working the Moscow–Brest line, and repeated the performance. Thereafter the Russian railwaymen acquired a
special prestige among revolutionaries.

From this period perhaps dates Pasternak's affection for railways and those who work them. He is always talking about
railways in his poems and short stories, and he gave a place of
honour to Pasha Antipov, the railway worker turned revolutionary, in *Doctor Zhivago*.

'Moscow in December' is a long, sustained elegy on the
betrayal and defeat of the insurrection. He describes the fierce
hopes of the revolutionaries at the beginning of the insurrection,
and how at the end their spirits were broken. Moscow is in
flames, and black smoke from the burning buildings hangs over
the city:

> *You would have said they were clouds, but they were black. Already
> they speak of an end of any resistance. The people are utterly weary,
> and inevitably they will turn to the right. 'Mein and Riemann.' At
> dawn a roar of thunder echoes along the boulevards. The Semyonovsky
> Regiment is transferred to the Brest line.*

> *Is it all over? All a fiasco? Is it the end? After the skirmishes,
> after the patrols, the night splitting asunder with cold, and the soldiers
> with Winchesters walking in sixes, the road running before them,
> licking the soles of their feet. And the garden close by freezes, rustling
> with icy silver. Time for renewed courage! In the hoops of the
> cannonade, like a nest of crows, the warehouses are set on fire; and
> revolving under the trees of a garden in flames, a maddened projectile
> lifts the roof from a house.*

> *By the light of the burning city, hastily, in Prokhorov's house, two
> men are shaving off their beards in a kitchen,[1] but what shall they gain
> by shaving? The fires float and swell in the air like the lather of soap
> on a shaving brush, and the night bursts into flame at the sound of the
> word: 'Mein!'*

[1] The reference is to Lenin and Vorovsky, who had entered Moscow
secretly early in December.

They are all hiding in the underground cellars, with no more strength to endure. From the factories comes the sound of growing despair. A white banner flaps from a flagpole. Why go to the hangman? Who goes there? The ringleaders, eh? The stamping of feet, and a scream like the whistle of wild boars. On the streets there is only certain death.

All hell has broken loose over there: but the sound of bullets subsides. Only the trembling of the wings of the snowstorm, and silence carving a deep furrow. Terrible is the silence: no flames, no gunfire. Smoke rises from the street, and out of the whirlwind come the Cossacks on horseback. Stop! Then interrogations, then searches. And then the patrol vanishes into the distance.

For the rest of his life Pasternak was to be deeply influenced by the December uprising, the smoke rising, the blood-stains in the snow. Again and again in his poems and in his prose writings he will return to those days when he first felt on his own body the whips of the enemy and saw a strange disfigured Moscow and heard the screams 'like the whistle of wild boars'. The impression made on him by the December uprising was so great that in later years it sometimes obscured the impression left by the October Revolution, twelve years later. For him December 1905 was a turning point, a vision, a time of extraordinary exaltation, a grace.

The Year Nineteen Five, with its mingled childhood memories and mature recollections, is a powerful but diffuse work. It has no centre. It wanders between Moscow, St. Petersburg and the Black Sea. It moves with such rapidity that the reader seems to be running breathlessly after the poet. Pasternak was aware of the lack of concentration in the work, and immediately after completing it he began to write a long series of poems about a single central character, the young Lieutenant Peter Schmidt who led a mutiny among the sailors at Sevastopol and almost singlehandedly seized a battle cruiser.

Lieutenant Schmidt was a man after Pasternak's heart. Handsome, intelligent, with a long narrow face and deep-set eyes under thick eyebrows, he looked the part of a young revolutionary to perfection. He had immense daring, and he had a gift for making declamatory statements which were almost poetry. The cruiser *Ochakov* was in the harbour at Sevastopol when he led the revolt, captured the ship, and telegraphed to the Tzar: I ASSUME COMMAND OF THE FLEET. SCHMIDT. Soon the mutiny spread along the docks, and ten more warships joined him. They steamed out of the harbour, only to be met by a superior force which effectively disposed of them. Schmidt jumped overboard, and was captured in the water. While he was in prison awaiting the verdict of the court-martial, no writing materials were permitted in his cell. He therefore wrote messages on the floor in candle grease. One of these messages read simply: *Soon the whole people will awake.* These words, remembered long after they were written, became the battle cry of the revolutionaries who followed him.

Schmidt acquitted himself well at the court-martial. He lectured his judges on the revolution, and promised that his attempted mutiny would be followed by many more, until at last the Tzarist naval forces would fall into the hands of the sailors. He was executed on March 6, 1906, at midnight, on the island of Berezan, together with three sailors who had taken part in the mutiny.

Pasternak's poem *Lieutenant Schmidt*, written in 1927, resembles a threnody. There are poems on every aspect of the revolt, but the poet writes throughout in a mood of sustained grief and sorrow over his death. Here is the lieutenant's last speech to his judges as rewritten by Pasternak:

> Vainly in days of chaos
> Men seek for a happy end.
> Some judge, and some repent.
> Some die on Golgotha.
>
> Like you I have my share
> In these tempestuous times:
> And I accept your verdict
> Without anger or complaint.
>
> I know you will not tremble
> To put a man to death.
> O martyrs of a dogma!
> O victims of the ages!

My love for Russia like a coat
Grew threadbare in these thirty years.
And now I neither pray nor hope
For any mercy.

These were the days you knew—
Those ever memorable days—
I saw myself plucked out of them
By the raging elements.

Terrible, if I had not been there
When my country rose!
Now I have no regrets
For the road I followed.

And yet I know the stake
On which I shall be bound
Forms the frontier between two ages.
I am grateful to have been chosen.

I am grateful to have been chosen. . . . It was a cry which
Pasternak was to repeat throughout his life, in sickness and
health, in triumph and defeat. To the very end of his life he
was to remain the quiet revolutionary.

THREE

The Wander Years

By the age of seventeen or eighteen Boris Pasternak's character was already formed. The influences which went to form his mind were already being absorbed. Tolstoy, Rilke, and Scriabin were to remain his idols—Tolstoy above all. In the fifty years that remained he would absorb other influences, submit to other disciplines, and assume some burdens which none of them could ever have contemplated, but it was from these three figures that he derived whatever strength poets derive from other poets. In his eyes Tolstoy, Rilke, and Scriabin were all supreme poets.

If he regarded Tolstoy more highly than any of the others, he had good reason to. The friendship between their families continued, and from time to time Leonid would announce that he was leaving for Yasnaya Polyana, and Boris would sometimes accompany him. Tolstoy's youngest daughter, Alexandra, still abundantly alive and working in New York, remembers him coming to the estate, a thin and dark-eyed boy who spoke rarely and had the gift of vanishing among shadows. Leonid too had this gift. He walked like a cat, and he would be busily sketching before Tolstoy realized that Leonid was in the room at all; then he would slip away, and some time later Leonid would appear from behind the trees in the garden and there would be more sketches while Tolstoy went for a walk. Though Leonid never achieved the great fame of Repin—he had begun as a magazine illustrator and some trace of journalism remained with him to the end—he had an uncanny knack of reproducing a likeness in a few quick strokes of his pencil.

Boris had none of his father's facility. Having renounced composition, he determined to be a poet, following the example of Rilke, whose books he found in his father's house one day when all the shelves were emptied for cleaning. There were stacks of books all over the floor, and quite by chance one of them, in a faded grey binding and with a dedicatory inscription to Leonid, fell at his feet. It was Rilke's *Mir zu Feier* ('In My Honour'), an early work written with a dazzling wealth of imagery which the poet was not to recapture until the last years of his life. Boris remembered that this was the German 'we left behind us one summer long ago on the whirling embankment of a forgotten station in the forests'. He ran to his father to make sure it was indeed the same person, and when this was confirmed, he shouted with joy. He was sixteen, still thinking of himself as a future composer. In the end it was largely the accidental discovery of the book with the faded grey binding which turned his thoughts to poetry.

Finding more books by Rilke, he devoured them eagerly. What delighted him most of all was Rilke's sense of dedication to poetry, his absolute urgency and purposefulness. Like Scriabin, Rilke was attempting to construct an entire universe out of his art. There was no decoration, unless the grave and fateful march of the verses could be called decoration; Rilke had something to say, and he said it with precision and a curious indifference to established usage. Like Scriabin, he seemed to have no ancestors.

Boris was deep in German literature. He read Kant and Hegel in his philosophy classes at the University; he enjoyed the poet Richard Dehmel; he was fascinated by Wagner, and had no sympathy for Nietzsche. He was attracted to the Russian poets Andrey Byely and Alexander Blok, who were at this time quarrelling violently—Byely was continually challenging Blok to duels. Boris's poems showed a closer relationship to those of Innokenty Annensky, a classical scholar and translator of Euripides, who published his poems under the pseudonym of *Nik. T.O.*, the letters forming the Russian word meaning 'no one'. Similar mysterious names were the order of the day. The circle of young poets to which Boris belonged called themselves the 'Serdarda'. No one could remember the origin of the word, until one of the poets remembered that he thought he had heard it on one of the Volga river steamers when the passengers were disembarking. The word was charming, meaningless, faintly Oriental, mysteriously significant, like much of the poetry which was being produced in Moscow at the time.

There were many groups of young poets in Moscow. They
expanded, coalesced, hovered in the air like soap bubbles, and
like soap bubbles they sometimes vanished without a trace.
Boris next joined the small group that had formed around Julian
Anissimov, a rich young poet, the son of a general, who lived
romantically in one of those ancient cottages which had survived from the time of Peter the Great; and in the cottage attic,
among the birds who had built their nests on the beams, the
poets gathered, recited their verses, played musical instruments,
painted, drank tea, and talked. The group was called 'Lyrika',
and Boris was inclined to regard it as a movement of Epigones,
meaning those who belonged to a tradition in decline. The
fearless new innovators were to come later.

He was living the normal life of a brilliant young student of
the University of Moscow, endlessly talking and debating, a
little theatrical, proud of his newly acquired learning, given to
vast theorizing. He was nineteen when he read a paper on
'Symbolism and Immortality' in the house of a friendly sculp-
tor, the audience sitting on the floor or peering down from a
gallery. There was the inevitable debate, and he defended
his thesis as well as he could, and though the paper is now
lost—he had a passion for losing his own writings—he seems
to have attached quite extraordinary value to it. Symbolism
and immortality were subjects close to his heart; they are the
theme of innumerable poems and many meditations in *Doctor
Zhivago*.

In the following year, on a bitterly cold November day,
Count Leo Tolstoy fled from Yasnaya Polyana to escape his
wife, whom he loved and hated. He was in full flight when
he fell ill on the train near Astapovo, and he was carried
into the stationmaster's house. Countess Tolstoy hurried after
him, but she was not permitted to see him until he was on
the verge of death. When he was dead, she took possession of
him.

By telegraph Countess Tolstoy summoned Leonid to paint
her husband on his deathbed, and with Leonid came Boris.
They entered the death room to find it deserted except for the
Countess, who wept and complained about all her sufferings
during those last days. As soon as she heard that her husband

had left the house, she tried to drown herself in a pond—a very shallow pond. She begged for sympathy, told about her attempt to commit suicide, and spoke of her eternal love for her husband. She seemed to be unaware that the room was filled with a storm cloud half the size of the sky, with lightning pouring out of it. It amazed Boris that the old Countess should be in such desperate need for sympathy at such a time. 'I loved him more than anyone else, I had more devotion for him, more understanding of him,' she whined, proclaiming her superiority over all the rivals to his affections, while Leonid unpacked his paintbox, and Boris marvelled that any woman, least of all the Countess, should join in pygmy battles in the presence of a dead giant.

There was something fearfully symbolic in the encounter between the dead Tolstoy and Boris Pasternak at the beginning of his career. It was as though the gods had deliberately chosen this way to hand on the torch of a great tradition.

While Leonid painted, Boris watched; and there was silence in the death chamber, for none of Tolstoy's immediate family was allowed to enter while the artist was at work. It was evening, and the setting sun formed a cross over the simple iron bed where Tolstoy lay in a peasant's blouse, one hand over his chest, small Christmas trees set around him, his face strangely peaceful and very small. A dead giant lay there, but to Boris he had assumed the shape of a little, wizened old man, one of those peasants who are described so minutely and so lovingly in the pages of his books; and it seemed perfectly appropriate that he should have died like a pilgrim by the roadside, while the indifferent trains flashed past, bearing away a host of obscure people who seemed almost to be the inventions of the dead novelist, for was he not the first to describe and understand them? In the eyes of Boris, the greatest virtue of Tolstoy lay precisely in that clairvoyant understanding, his penetrating power of entering their souls. 'All his life, and at every instant of his life, this moralist possessed the gift of being able to see things *absolutely*, in their depths and in relief, as sometimes but very rarely we see things in childhood, or at moments of overwhelming joy, or in the triumph of great spiritual victories.' So Boris wrote in the last years of his life, in a slender autobiographical fragment intended as an introduction to his collected poems, but there was never any period when he did not hold fast to the belief that Tolstoy was the greatest Russian of them all.[1]

On the following day he was still in Astapovo. He watched the students carrying the coffin across the garden of the station-master's house and saw it put into a freight car. He heard the singing of the lament on the station platform, and saw the train disappearing into the distance, and returned to Moscow.

Moscow was philosophy, the coffee houses on the Tverskoy Boulevard, the companionship of brilliant young men, love affairs, flower markets, the endless pursuit of the unattainable. Rasputin was already exerting his influence on the Russian court. Diaghilev was the acknowledged emperor of ballet. Pavlova, Karsavina, and Nijinsky were in the full flood of their success. Moscow and St. Petersburg were the centres of a fastidious and exotic culture. The last giddy days of the autocracy seemed to derive from another age than that which produced Dostoevsky, Chekhov and Tolstoy. The end was not very far away.

Boris lived like thousands of other university students of the time. He took cheap furnished lodgings, did some private tutoring, led some adult education classes, where for the first time he came in contact with clerks, office workers and ordinary workmen, and took very little thought of money. It was not that money had no attractions for him; it was simply that money was irrelevant, for one could live very cheaply in Moscow and it never occurred to him that there was any advantage in amassing wealth.

His amusements were simple ones. He liked the circus. He liked long lonely walks through the city, and he haunted the flower markets, where he became drunk on the profusion of flowers imported from Italy—'flaming rows of peonies, yellow marguerites, tulips and anemones, all wrestling with one another'. Characteristically he preferred the narcissi, those flowers which are 'diluted to the purest whiteness', with their

---

[1] In a letter written shortly before his death to Robert Miller, the editor of *Fellowship*, Pasternak wrote: 'Tolstoy's *Hadji Murat* is a little close universe for itself. But *Anna Karenina* is a carefully accomplished research on a corner of Russian society of a certain definite time. The first is marvelous and superhuman. The second without wonders and conforming to rule.'

promise of an eternal springtime. In these massed flowers he was disposed to see evidence of renewal and resurrection. Like Dostoevsky, who was also deeply impressed by the ancient Greek myths, he saw in the flowers the abiding presence of the earth-goddess. 'It was as though their very scent, which hovered and then vanished away, reminded me of something and at the same time cheating the mind, permitted the spring months to create that concept of the earth which won them back to life year after year; and the sources of the Greek myth of Demeter seemed to be very close at hand.'

But in those exciting years in which he was still finding himself, there were many other mythologies to attract him. In particular there were those mythologies attached to the medieval cities in Europe where learning quietly flourished. His father had learned painting in Munich, and he was determined to see Germany. But how do you travel abroad when you are a penniless student of philosophy?

One blustery rainy day in February 1912, Boris's close friend, the young and erratic Dmitry Samarin, suddenly began to enlarge on the fantastic beauty of the German city of Marburg, all gables and medieval courtyards and narrow winding streets. Boris knew, of course, that Marburg University was the centre of a new school of philosophy presided over by Professor Hermann Cohen, a man with a brain like a battering ram, famous for his wit and his devastating powers of analysis. But no one had ever described to him before the attractions of this ancient Hessian city not far from the French frontier. They were sitting in one of the cafés on the Tverskoy Boulevard; Samarin was munching a biscuit; the rain pelted outside; and suddenly Boris was aware of the overwhelming beauty of this city, which had given a new lease of life to philosophy. The conversation turned to Stendhal, but Boris continued to be obsessed with his vision of Marburg. 'I was filled with a feeling of deep regret for this precious city which, as it seemed to me, I had no more hope of seeing than I could hope to see my own ears.'

A month passed, and then one morning in April his mother told him she had saved 200 rubles from her piano lessons, and she hoped he would spend it on travel. He had no strength to refuse and jumped at the opportunity. He ran to one of the bookshops on the Mokhovaya, near the University, and was able to buy a copy of the syllabus for the summer course at Marburg University: those were the days when the European universities were continually exchanging information about their courses. He read the syllabus avidly, decided what courses to take, worked out his expenses, and early the next month set out for Marburg by train. In Poland the apple trees were blossoming, and Berlin, where he changed trains, was a city of young men 'who had received only the day before gifts of swords, helmets, pipes, real bicycles and frock coats, just like grown-ups'. For two successive nights Boris remained wide awake, in a state of constantly growing exaltation and excitement.

Marburg was even more desirable than he had hoped. Everything about the place delighted him, from the crenellated walls of the castle to the street called the Barfüsserstrasse, along which the medieval Franciscan monks strode barefoot. A famous legend was associated with Marburg. Elizabeth of Hungary was living in the city, practising her saintly devotions against the will of her harsh confessor, Conrad of Marburg, who forbade her to minister to the sick and the poor. God, in His infinite mercy, therefore brought about a snowstorm, and under cover of the storm Elizabeth continued her ministrations. Boris liked the story so well that he included it in his autobiography, spinning around the figure of Saint Elizabeth the same shining gossamer that he was to spin later around the figure of Larissa Guishar in *Doctor Zhivago*.

Long, long ago, when that first January ushered in the perfectly normal year—it was the twelve hundred and thirtieth of our era—a living historic figure, Elizabeth of Hungary, stepped down from Marburg Castle.

All this happened at a point so far away in time that when the imagination reaches out toward it, it encounters a snowstorm, which arises out of the increasing cold by virtue of the laws governing the conquest of the unattainable. At this point night sets in, the hills clothe themselves in forests, and in the forests the wild beasts roam. Morality and custom are thickly encrusted with ice.

The future saint was canonized only three years after her death. Her confessor was a tyrant; that is to say, a man without imagination. This sober man of affairs saw that the penances imposed upon her in the confessional only lifted her into a state of ecstasy. In search of penances which would be truly unbearable to her, he forbade her to help the sick and the poor. And here legend takes the place of history, for it appears that such self-denial was beyond her powers and therefore to whiten her sin of disobedience a snowstorm concealed her as she made her way to the lower town, and for the duration of her nocturnal ministrations the storm changed her bread into flowers.

So is Nature sometimes compelled to depart from her own laws, when a fervent tyrant insists too firmly on imposing his own laws. It matters not that the voice of natural law is clothed in miracle: in a religious age a miracle is a sign of authenticity.

The celebration of Saint Elizabeth comes strangely from a poet writing in communist Russia in the late twenties, but the last paragraph provides the clue to his motive. Here Pasternak is speaking quietly, with full voice, against the demands of dictatorship. The face of Conrad of Marburg gives place to the face of Lenin, or any communist dictator.

But life in Marburg did not consist exclusively of the contemplation of saints and tyrannical confessors. There were lectures to be attended, convivial meetings at cafés with students from all over the world, among them a young revolutionary from Barcelona who was continually declaiming the verses of Verlaine. Boris had a small room in the Gysselbergstrasse on the outskirts of the city, overlooking a henhouse made from an antiquated tramcar, from which the wheels had been removed. The boarding house was presided over by an old woman suffering from goitre. She was a Prussian, stern and punctilious, very pious, as far removed as possible from the intellectual fevers of the University as she gazed uncomprehendingly at her charges, whose strange behaviour she regarded as a punishment for her sins.

Pasternak's behaviour was not calculated to calm her. He

studied at all hours of the day and night, brought strange guests
to his barren room, and sometimes vanished without a word of
explanation.

One day in August two Russian girls who were sisters came
to stay briefly in Marburg. They were the daughters of a
wealthy merchant. Boris had been their tutor in Moscow, and
was passionately in love with the elder one and half in love with
the younger. Abandoning classes, he spent three reckless days
wandering with them in the streets of Marburg and in the surrounding countryside. On the last day, when they were about
to leave for Berlin, he fell into a profound melancholy. He
could not bear to live without them. Especially he could not
bear to live without the elder girl, and he begged her to marry
him. Distraught, ill at ease, he advanced upon her, so that she
was forced back against the wall, where she uttered the words
he thought he would never hear. Still hoping she would change
her mind, wholly at the mercy of the two girls, he accompanied
them to the railway station. When the train was already moving, he was unable to bear the pain of separation and jumped
on it. In *The Safe Conduct* he relates his adventures on the train
and later in Berlin with admirable restraint:

I ran beside the train, and at the end of the platform, when
it was going at full speed, I leap on the running board. The
heavy door at the end of the coach had not been slammed to.
An excited conductor barred my way, at the same time supporting me with one arm around my shoulder, as though he
feared my determination to commit suicide would not survive his remonstrances. My friends hurried out into the
corridor, and thrust notes into the conductor's hand for my
rescue and for my fare. He relented, and I followed the two
sisters into their compartment, and so we rushed headlong to
Berlin. The fairy-tale holiday, which had almost ended
disastrously, continued with scarcely an interruption, intensi-
fied tenfold by the frenzied motion of the train and by the
blissful headache, the reward of my experiences.

I had jumped onto the train simply to say good-bye, but
now once more I forgot this inevitable duty, and only remembered it when it was too late. I had barely come to my senses

when I discovered that the day was over, evening had come, and the reverberating roof of the Berlin terminus was pressing down on us. The sisters were to be met at the station. It was undesirable that they should be seen with me in my agitated condition. They convinced me that we had said good-bye, and I had merely failed to notice it. I vanished in the crowd, amid the gaseous uproar of the station.

It was night, and an evil drizzle was falling. I had no business to be in Berlin. The next train for Marburg did not leave until early the next morning, and I could easily have waited at the station, but felt no desire to be among those crowds of people. My features were convulsed, tears kept welling up in my eyes, and my thirst for one final farewell remained unquenched.

His first serious love affair had come to an end in ignominious defeat. He spent the night wandering around Berlin from one cheap lodging house to another, until at last he found one which would accept him, unkempt and luggageless as he was. It was a night of pure horror, and he spent it sitting by the table in a nauseating little room, staring into space, at the end of his strength and in danger of going mad. The next day he made the journey to Marburg like a man riding through a nightmare. The landlady opened the door and suggested that it might be better if he gave due warning in future if he absented himself overnight, and when he explained that sudden business had called him to Berlin, she shook her head as though she were dealing with a madman. In compensation there was a postcard from Hermann Cohen, the great philosopher, inviting him to one of those famous Sunday dinners to which only the most favoured students were invited. There was also a letter from a girl cousin saying she was staying for a few days in Frankfurt and hoped to see him there. He had to choose between going to the dinner and seeing his cousin. It was an easy choice. He went to Frankfurt.

When he returned to Marburg, he had made up his mind. He would abandon philosophy forever. It was not in the least that Hermann Cohen had failed him—he had nothing but the most absolute devotion to that fat, stocky philosopher with the deep-set eyes and the flaring moustaches—but he had discovered that poetry claimed him to the exclusion of everything else. He went to see the professor to bid him farewell. There was some talk of Boris returning to Marburg to take his doctorate, but nothing came of it. They were walking slowly along the street, the old white-haired philosopher jabbing his cane against the flagstones, and sometimes the cane would pause there as though waiting for something to happen. It was the triviality of Scriabin which had prevented Boris from following in his path; now he was ashamed of his own platitudes as he spoke of his plans for the future, watching the cane which was acting as a kind of barometer to the older man's feelings, and being dreadfully intimidated by it.

With his remaining money he fled to Italy. He stayed briefly at Pisa, then went on to Venice, where he fell helplessly in love with the Piazza San Marco. Venice was a golden lake, alive and quivering, fed by innumerable springs, perhaps the original lake of creation. Venice dazzled with its bounty, its excessive beauty, its stern attachment to the arts. He found lodgings near the Academia, wandered from one mysterious square to another, sauntered through a hundred churches, and found himself drowning contentedly in paintings which he had already studied in reproduction, but now they dazzled and thundered from the very walls where they had been painted. He admired Carpaccio and Bellini, paid tribute to Veronese and Titian, and reserved his utmost homage for Tintoretto. Seeing those naked bodies towering on the walls of churches, it pleased him to remember an apocryphal story told of Pope Julius II, who complained that the figures on the ceiling of the Sistine Chapel were not clothed sumptuously. 'How could they be?' Michelangelo is supposed to have said. 'In those days people were not decked out in gold. The people I have depicted were poor.'

Instead of Germanic philosophy there was a riot of colour, the sense of artistic accomplishment flowing through the ages and along the canals, where the gondolas plied and the steamboats chugged merrily. He saw the churches as anchored ships, their sails open to all the breezes of heaven, and there was a freshness about the place which suggested that it came to birth yesterday. Astonishment gave place to understanding, and understanding to love, as he contemplated the miraculous abundance which the city had produced almost without effort. He saw that the Bible was a picture book with pictures which inevitably change over the ages, and that it was perfectly possible for the men of the Renaissance to combine the utmost spirituality with the utmost licence, believing intensely in the physical world and in the resurrection—for the first time he introduced the theme of the resurrection which lies at the heart of *Doctor Zhivago*. 'Italy,' he wrote, 'crystallized for me all that we unconsciously breathe from our cradles.' He found himself sympathizing with the Englishmen who bade farewell to that perfect piazza with all the sorrow and all the physical contortions which go with bidding farewell to the beloved. 'As everyone knows, there is no European culture which approaches the Italian so closely as the English.'

He was like a famished child, eating hungrily. Venice was a revelation of beauty so overwhelming that he was continually catching his breath; and he was just as dazzled by the quiet squares in the remote regions of the city as by the sumptuous palaces, 'where there are no empty spaces, because everything is brimming with beauty'.

On his last night he attended a concert in the Piazza San Marco, and years later he attempted to record his excitement when a sudden shower of fireworks illuminated the night sky:

The façades of the buildings were clothed from head to foot in little lamps. Around three sides there glowed a black and white transparency. Under the open sky the faces of the audience were drenched in a watery clarity, as if in a magnificently illuminated ballroom. Suddenly from the fictitious ceiling of the ballroom there descended a gentle sprinkle of rain, but this soom came to an end, giving place to a shower of another kind. The reflection of fireworks simmered above the piazza in the many-coloured darkness. The bell tower of San Marco cut like a red marble rocket into the rosy mist, which rose in wreathes halfway to the top. And a little further away dark purple vapours circled in streams, lapping the five-domed shell of the Cathedral as in a fairy tale. That end of the piazza might well have been a kingdom below the

D

seas. On the portico of the Cathedral four spanking horses shone gold, having galloped there from ancient Greece, coming to an abrupt pause as on the edge of a precipice.

Like the golden horses, he too was coming to an abrupt pause on the edge of a precipice. He returned to Russia filled with the determination to be a poet, but with no idea how he would make a living. He passed his final examination at Moscow University, spent a brief holiday with his parents in the country, and then set out to take the world by storm with the immature verses he had written in Marburg and during his travels in Italy. But the world refused to be taken by storm, his parents could no longer provide for him, and he continued to eke out a small living as a tutor. The great German poet Friedrich Hölderlin had spent the best years of his life as a tutor, and he had been broken by the experience.

Among those who came to his rescue was the Lithuanian poet Jurgis Baltrushaitis, who owned a large estate on the Oka river near the town of Alexin, where Chekhov had written many of his stories The town was a few miles north of Tula. Baltrushaitis was a gifted poet and literary director of the newly founded Kamerny Theatre in Moscow. Rich, immensely talented in his friendships, at the mercy of an ungovernable melancholy which showed itself in his verses, he liked to surround himself with poets and artists, and he was especially close to Vyacheslav Ivanov, one of the few Russian poets of the time who possessed an authentic genius. Ivanov was a small man with flaming red hair, a sharp nose, and an impulsive genial manner. That summer—it was the summer of 1914—he was staying on the estate, and for the first time Boris, who was tutoring the son of Jurgis Baltrushaitis, came in close contact with the Symbolist movement. The air was heady with poetry. Konstantin Balmont, another authentic poet, was living nearby. There were constant discussions about poetry, and one day Boris showed his poems collected together under the title *A Twin in the Clouds*—it was one of those meaningless titles fashionable among poets at the time—to Maria Baltrushaitis, the wife of his host. She read them carefully, and said: 'You'll be sorry to have published them one day.' He did publish them, and afterward he was sorry. He was one of those poets who develop late. It was three years before the storm of poetry broke in him, and then it came in full flood.

In July 1914, he was summoned to Moscow to take his medical examination, but was given 'the white ticket' with complete exemption from military service, because one of his legs was shorter than the other. He spent the late summer as tutor in the house of Moritz Philippe, a wealthy merchant of German origin, and when the house was looted during the anti-German riots, he escaped with his life and his clothes, losing his books and manuscripts. It was 'the last summer when life appeared to pay heed to individuals, and when it was easier to love than to hate'.

Inevitably he was swept into war work. Having no mechanical gifts of any kind, he became a clerk in obscure factories far behind the lines, deep in the interior of European Russia, on the frontiers of Asia. He spent most of these years in the Ural Mountains, or in the factory towns along the banks of the deep-flowing Kama River, which enters the Volga not far from Kazan. The sharp, craggy Urals fascinated him, and for the first time he felt he was penetrating into the heart of Russia. He never lost his affection for these frontier lands, returning to them again and again in his poems and in the chapters in *Doctor Zhivago* dealing with the Civil War. For a while he was a roving commissioner attached to the draft boards, and it pleased him to remember that he was able to free innumerable factory workers from military service. The Urals are immensely rich in minerals, and all the factories were being converted into munition plants.

The war was a long way away, and news came rarely. He seemed to be living in some remote backwater where time stood still. Nothing had changed since the early nineteenth century, and there were Tartar villages where the traditions of the fifteenth century were still maintained. In winter the mail came by horse-drawn sleigh from Kazan, two hundred miles away.

He was still working in the Urals when the February Revolution broke out in St. Petersburg. At once he decided to leave for Moscow, making the journey by sleigh through the snow-covered forests with a single companion. It was like travelling through fairyland: the trees all white, and the snowdrifts piled high, and the stars peering through the snow-laden branches at the lonely land. There were relay-stations which had remained unaltered since the Middle Ages, lost in an immensity of whiteness. They would stay long enough to change horses and drink tea from the steaming samovars, and then once again they were racing through the forest roads toward Moscow.

In Moscow, in the excitement of that summer, while the revolution gathered strength and the Tzardom perished to give place to a hitherto unknown form of government, he found himself as a poet.

FOUR

Ten Poems

The clearest, most memorable and most important fact about art is its conception, and the world's finest works of art, those which tell of the most diverse things, in reality tell us of their own birth.

WHEN Boris Pasternak wrote those lines in his autobiography, *The Safe Conduct*, he was demonstrating his adherence to the code long since established by the Symbolists. According to this code a work of art exists in its own right and is concerned only with its own flowering; its validity lies within itself, and it has no aim except to please itself. So Mallarmé might have written, after composing poems which seem to have been chiselled out of stars and ice and the immense spaces of the universe.

But in fact although Pasternak often wrote about poetry in this way, and always reserved for himself the right to speak in a private language, his manner of writing poetry has little in common with the Symbolists. From the beginning—from the summer of 1917 when he found himself as a poet—he was concerned with the tangible earth, with nature in all her moods, with the human condition in all its amazing variety. He remains a difficult poet because his vision is intricate and conveyed with an extraordinary density of imagery. He defies translation; and no one has yet succeeded in conveying in English the richness of his vocabulary, the leaping brilliance of his rhythms, the way he gives the impression of writing in a language he has invented this morning. Yet no one could be more tradition-bound. His verse patterns are the simplest imaginable. Unlike his contemporaries, Andrey Byely, Vladimir Mayakovsky and Velimir Khlebnikov, who were always experimenting with language, inventing new words and changing the forms of existing words, Pasternak instinctively recoiled from experiment.

He believed that the Russian language was so rich that everything anyone wanted to say could be said in it. 'I never understood what they were trying to do,' he wrote later. 'It seemed to me that the most surprising discoveries in language were made when the artist was drunk with his subject, and suddenly, without time for reflection, he uttered the fresh word in the ancient language without for a moment asking himself whether he was writing something new or old.' As Pasternak saw it, if there was to be a revolution in poetry, it should be one of feeling rather than words. His task as a poet was to sharpen his sensibilities to the point where they were equipped to deal with the most remote, the most tenuous, the most delicate resources of the human spirit.

Inevitably his work is extremely personal, complex and close-knit, but the complexities and close texture of his verse do not arise from any deliberate singularity of vision; they derive from the nature of the hunt. He is a huntsman armed with some wickedly sharp weapons and with nets which are intricately woven. He darts about in the forest, creating his own light, throwing sudden beams at the quarry, catching it in unexpected postures, which are unexpected only because we have never observed them so closely before, for we recognize the truth of what he has described once he has explained it to us. He wanders through the forest which is the familiar forest of the human soul, but he takes the unfamiliar roads. There is a sense in which all his poems are descriptions of the soul at bay, caught in a shining light.

His range is immense, as it must be if a man chooses to write about the human soul in all its peregrinations. There are love poems of extraordinary savagery; poems of mockery; poems which attempt to capture whole cities and nations on a single page; poems like the humming of telegraph wires; poems like explosions of dynamite. A great deal of what he had to say is contained in his two books *My Sister Life* and *Themes and Variations*, the first written during the summer of 1917, the second during the crowded years of the Civil War. During much of this time he starved even while holding a position as a librarian or as an assistant in a bookshop. But it is only rarely that the agony of these years is reflected in his poems. Rarely moved by

historical events, he continued to write about the vast subtleties
of the human soul.

Here, for example, is one of the early poems which describes
by a series of subtle and deliberate improvisations the long
summer lull before the storm which burst in October.

SUMMER 1917

Thirst strains for butterflies,
For moths, for household stains.
All round are woven memories
Of honey, mint and summer.

No clocks chime, but the ringing flails
From dawn to early dusk
Assert their dreams of stings
In this enchanted weather.

The sunset strolling leisurely
Yields to the cicadas,
While stars and woods surrender
Powder to gardens and kitchens.

The moon spreads its long beams
Or vanishes in deep shade.
Softly, softly the night shines,
Flowing shyly from cloud to cloud.

More from their dreams than from roofs,
More in forgetfulness than shyness
The small rain shuffles to the door
Where the air smells of wine corks.

The smell of dust, the smell of grass.
And should we pay them tribute,
The smell of gentry's teaching was
Of brotherhood and freedom.

The councils met in villages:
You over there, did you attend them?
Bright with wood sorrel hung the days
When the air smelled of wine corks.

What Pasternak has done in the space of seven short verses is
to suggest an entire summer melting away before the threaten-
ing storm. There are hints of menace in the ringing flails with

their dreams of stings, and the sun strolls a little too leisurely for comfort. The moon vanishes, and the small rain falls, and the vision of peace has thinned down until it is no more than a whiff of convivial wine, but with what delicate artistry he has conveyed the scene, what controlled passion informs it! In the penultimate verse he introduces casually the village councils or *zemstvas* which were busily debating the future of the country, giving them their proper place in the fading light. There is no excitement; only a brooding melancholy in the flaming wood sorrel, the sense of the year straining toward its end.

In the original Russian, of course, it is not quite so simple. To convey the mood Pasternak uses heavy words with slow-moving vowels: half rhymes and assonance are continually slowing up the meter. There is even an untranslatable *double-entendre*, for *babochki* means 'butterflies', but it can also mean 'young women'. There is a deliberate quickening beginning with the second line of the penultimate verse. But what is important is that Pasternak has succeeded in creating a memorable poem out of the least likely objects—household stains, moths and wine corks. With a conjuror's deftness he has transformed them into visionary heartbeats.

All through Pasternak's verses there is a concentration on what Wordsworth called 'modes of being'. In one of his least satisfactory early poems he attempted to offer a definition of poetry:

> It is a steeply crescendoing whistle,
> It is icicles broken and ringing,
> It is night and the frozen leaves,
> It is the debate between nightingales. . . .

For him poetry was all these things, but it was also very much more. These words only suggest the kind of language he delighted to use: words which were sharp and piercing, clanging like ice, gentle as nightingales. But the words are only the tools fashioned for the purpose of exploring the secret places of the soul.

Words were the tools, but images which he called 'miracles in a word' gave them their cutting edge. He would pile image on image with dazzling effect. He would cut short an image in

full flight, bind it abruptly to another image of an entirely
different kind and then set them spinning across the sky amid a
swarm of other images until all these images coalesced into a
single shower of dazzling fireworks. In one of his most famous
poems he attempts to describe Pushkin at the moment of
creating his fiercely passionate poem, *The Prophet*. There is no
conventional portrait of Pushkin at work. Instead there is a
portrait of the turmoil in his soul, all space and all the great
places of the earth waiting in attendance on him. He is sitting
alone in a room, writing by the light of a guttering candle, while
the night races headlong into the dawn:

> Stars swarmed. Headlands washed in the sea.
> Salt sprays blinding. Tears have grown dry.
> Darkness brooded in bedrooms. Thoughts swarming,
> While the Sphinx listens patiently to the Sahara.
>
> Candles guttered. Blood, it seems, lay frozen
> In the huge Colossus. Lips were swelling
> Into the perfect blue smile of the desert.
> Night faded with the ebbing of the tide.
>
> Winds from Morocco stirred the sea. Simoons roared.
> Archangel snored amid the muffled snows.
> Candles guttered. The first text of *The Prophet*
> Dried, and on the Ganges rose the dawn.

It is a poem which can be read on many levels, but on all its
levels it moves with the effect of inevitability. There have been
many attempts to interpret it, to distinguish the meaning of
each image. Perhaps the blinding salt sprays represent the
tumultuous energy of poetic creation; perhaps the Colossus is
the Sphinx, and both of them are Pushkin; perhaps the winds
from Morocco represent a lull in creation, and the roaring of
the simoons a renewed outburst of energy which dies away in
the northern snows. One critic has suggested that the Colossus
represents the poet's state when his work begins, the listening
Sphinx his expectant consciousness on the verge of starting, the
swelling lips his joy as the work expands. But there is no need
to tear the butterfly to tatters. Miraculously, Pasternak has
conveyed the urgency of creation by a dazzling display of
images: a blaze of images cascading into one another, all in

their proper order and all at the right time. The violence is wonderfully controlled; each small group of words is compact with energy and colour; the pace is so furious that the reader has no time to pause for breath. In twelve lines there are sixteen images. Yet the poem is in no sense a virtuoso piece. Examined coldly, when the rush of excitement is over, it suggests a carefully constructed mosaic, with every coloured fragment exactly in place.

There is a similar explosion of imagery, and an even faster pace, in one of the love poems he composed in 1918, belonging to a series called *The Separation*. For the most part they are poems of anguish and terror, but one stands out among the rest with a vision of headlong joy in love-making:

> Weave the shower like waves of cool elbows,
> Like lilies all satin and strong, with failing hands!
> Flee to the fields! Exult! O catch them, for in
>   the furious chase
> The clamorous woods are choked with the echo of hunts
>   in Calydon,
> Where like a roe Actaeon heedless pursues Atalanta
> Into the meadows where they love in the fathomless
>   blue,
> Whistling by the ears of horses, and kissing
> To the impetuous baying of the chase, caressing
> To the pealing of horns and the cracking of trees,
>   hooves and claws.
> Oh, into the fields! Into the open! Like these!

In the Russian original the pace is even swifter, and the long lines have the effect of sliding along sibilants, gathering pace as they go. Nowhere else has Pasternak succeeded so brilliantly in conveying the flight of young lovers into each other's arms.

Such poems are rare in Pasternak's work: his mood is usually more contemplative, more cautious, more intricately woven into a kind of meditative melancholy. Like a Chinese sage, he will stand in his garden and absorb it piece by piece until he becomes the garden. The rain falls, and the dust forms little pellets like iron balls sprinkled with powder. He notices the parched rye turning a brilliant red 'like a hairy erysipelas'. These words have a raw look in English, but they are not raw in

Russian, and there is no denying the accuracy of the observer's
eye. He has the hawk's eye, and sees minutely; and when the
eye opens wide the small garden becomes the whole universe.

THE SULTRY NIGHT

The small rain fell, but did not bend
The grasses in the thunder's belly:
Dust only swallowed up the rain
In pellets: iron in a silent powder.

The village hoped for no relief,
The poppies lay in depths of swoon,
And while the rye grew fever-red,
A hairy erysipelas, the gods went raving mad.

All through the orphaned, sleepless wastes
Of world-wide dreary emptiness
The screams flew headlong from the posts,
The whirlwind died, and then lay still.

Close after them a few faint drops
Went blind; the wet boughs broke
In open quarrel with the famished wind.
My heart grew tense. They spoke of me.

I felt the fearful chattering garden was
An endless never-stopping thing;
And while the shrubs and shutters spoke,
I went unnoticed in the street.

If they see me, there's no going back.
They'll go on chattering to the end of time!

In 'The Sultry Night' Pasternak is describing a mood—a
mood which involves a love affair with the physical earth, of
terror and affection culminating in a knowledge of earth's
indifference to her lover—which we recognize readily, but no
one had ever stated the case for the lover with such passionate
detachment before. The poem, which appears at first to be so
complex, proves to be completely lucid, and completely new.
It is not only that the poet is saying things which have never
been said, but one would have thought they were unsayable.
He is saying something which is intensely personal, and at the
same time universal.

Not all his poems are of this kind. Sometimes he will speak about a well-remembered place, and out of long contemplation extract from his memories only what was most essential and meaningful. Once in 1918 he found himself in the small village of Spasskoye outside Moscow, and saw a house in a park deserted by its patrician owners, crumbling away. In the poem he wrote shortly afterward the house becomes many things. It becomes absence; it becomes death; it becomes the repository for the poet's vain longing for the security of the past, and at the same time it is the symbol of all that has been cast away by the Bolshevik Revolution. It is all this, and more, for it is also a very real house accurately and lovingly seen.

THE HOUSE AT SPASSKOYE

This memorable September is strewn over Spasskoye:
Surely it is the time to leave the house alone!
Beyond the palings Echo roars to the herdsman,
And in the woods the sound of an axe rings clear.

The shivering marshes in the park last night:
The reappearing sun went out a moment later.
The harebells will not drink rheumatic dews.
Now the lilac dropsy stains the birchwoods.

Sad, sad the woods. Longing for rest,
Under the snows, the unwaking slumber of bear dens:
The trees among stumps beyond the blackened palings
Gape like a black-bordered obituary.

More faded and diseased the birchwoods every day,
Thinning out within the watery shade—
He mumbles: You are fifteen years old now,
And, O my child, what do we do with them?

They are so many—nothing to joke about—
Like birds in bushes, and mushrooms in hedges:
Too often we have curtained our horizon,
And hidden all our distances in mist.

On his deathbed the typhus-ridden clown
Hears from the gallery the gods' Homeric laughter.
So from Spasskoye we behold hallucinations
Of the old timbered house in its mortal agony.

We do not have to ask who 'the typhus-ridden clown' is, for it is evidently the poet wandering in the shadowland. This poem, which might be called 'Autumn 1918', provides a sequel to 'Summer 1917', and perhaps consciously Pasternak employs some of the same devices. In the earlier poem we hear the ominous ringing of the flails, as here we hear the ringing of the axe. There is the same detached, affectionate observance of nature. Suddenly the detachment gives way, and in the lines

> Sad, sad the woods. Longing for rest,
> Under the snows, the unwaking slumber of bear dens:

we are made aware that the poet is talking with the voice of the woodland. There was hope in 'Summer 1917'. There is very little hope left in 'The House at Spasskoye'.

Paternak never apologized for his acutely personal vision. He never shouted like Mayakovsky, whose later verses sometimes sound like the roaring of a mob, or screamed like Essenin, who was continually comparing himself to God and inventing vast exalted images. Pasternak's themes are houses, gardens, clouds, the grass growing between the flagstones, the bird perching on a branch in the rain, a railway train lumbering through the night. He saw the world as it is, and had no faith that it could be changed by revolutionary movements. He even said as much in his introductory poem to *My Sister Life*, which includes a famous verse describing the poet with a muffler around his throat and shielding himself with the palm of his hand as he cries across the courtyard: 'Dear ones, what millennium are you celebrating out there?'

ABOUT THESE VERSES

Along the pavement I will grind
The dust into the sunlit glass:
In winter-time I'll open wide the ceiling,
And let the reeking corners read my lines.

My garrets shall be declamations
And bows to wintry window-panes,
While snowdrifts, wonders, agonies
Will leapfrog up until they reach the roof.

The snows will never sweep the moon away:
They'll settle on the last and opening pages.
Then I'll remember: There's the sun in the sky.
I'll see the world has long since changed.

Christmas like a hawk will stare:
Walk-wandering days shall be my conversations,
Speaking of all the things that are
Unknown to my beloved and to me.

With a muffler round my throat,
Shielding myself with the palm of my hand,
I'll shout across the courtyard: 'Dear ones,
What millennium are you celebrating out there?'

Who cleared that pathway to my door,
That hole all choked with sleet and snow,
While I was smoking with Lord Byron
And drinking wine with Edgar Allan Poe?

These lines are a declaration of independence. In effect, Pasternak is saying that he will retreat into the empty house and continue to write verses in spite of the tumultuous storms outside. He is perfectly prepared to remain defenceless: the storm will blow the muffler away, the hand may be cut off, he will still write. But to take the verses literally, as they must be taken, is to forget that they are also deliberately ironic. He does not say: 'Tyrants, what millennium are you celebrating out there?' He says: 'Dear ones . . .' and employs the most tender of all Russian words of affection.

The irony is passionate, even savage. There is indignation in it, but only enough to fill a wine cup. As usual, his mood is constantly changing, and though he salutes the communists from an ironic distance—'What millennium are you celebrating out there?'—he almost commends them for clearing a pathway to his door. There is nothing simple in the poem unless it is his picture of the house becoming a mouth which utters his verses.

There is a little more savagery in a poem he wrote some years later addressed to a friend, whose identity is not revealed, though it is just possible that Stalin is intended.

TO A FRIEND

Surely I know, while stumbling in the dark,
Our night will never brighten in a dawn.
Am I a monster? Do I care at all
Whether the fate of millions is assuaged?

Surely I know the Five Year Plan is mine—
With it I fall, and with it rise again.
Then why disown my thoughts? and why deny
My own inertia? Should it be otherwise?

In vain in these days of the Great Soviet
When power is handed over to Authority,
A special seat is given to the poet.
If it is not empty, it is dangerous.

The trap is set in the last line. He is not saying only that the poet has no place in the council chambers; he is saying that poetry would become poison if it sat in the seat of authority. Once again he is proclaiming the independence of the poet— gently, menacingly and without any thought of the consequences.

It was scarcely possible for him to look on poetry otherwise. From very early days he was immersed in a fierce partisan battle for integrity of poetic expression. Ultimately the poem must deal with the real world; it must be accurate; it must speak from the heart. To permit the air to flow into the poem, the emotion may be set against a landscape, but the landscape itself must have a definite relevance to the emotion. Finally the poem must be written in strict metrical form, and there must be no arbitrariness. Neither Pasternak nor those who saw poetry with his eyes showed any interest in the violent poetic experiments which came into existence after the first World War.

They asked for precision, lucidity, a certain calm, a certain sustained violence. Here for example is an early poem by Anna Akhmatova, who became a close friend of Pasternak and was famous for her classic purity of expression:

Thank God, I very rarely dream of you.
No longer do I see you everywhere.
The mist is rising on the sandy road,
And shadows flit upon the silent water.

All day long the pealing of bells
Over the endless spaces of ploughed land:
Standing here, the bells are heard best,
And best is the view of the monastery.

I strip the branches off the lilac bushes—
Those that are no longer blossoming.
Along the ancient earthen ramparts
Two monks are walking patiently.

In this familiar world of shapes and colours,
O bring me life to feast my blinded eyes.
There is an ice-cold calm within my soul
Since God has healed it of love's fever.

Poems very similar to this were written by Pasternak to the
end of his life. He shares with Anna Akhmatova an extraordinary sense of empathy with nature: his clouds, his roads and
rivers and fruit trees and fences are all designed to reflect the
emotions, but they are nevertheless accurate descriptions of
things seen. Pasternak goes beyond Anna Akhmatova in the
deliberate violence of his imagery. His monks do not walk
patiently, his church bells do not simply fill the empty space
above ploughed fields. Anna Akhmatova describes an evening
in terms of the mist rising and the shadows flitting; there is no
sun. Pasternak sees the evening at sunset, and his emotions are
coloured by drops of ruby fire, and the sailor's chest is 'stamped
with scarlet wax'. Pasternak has the painter's eye, and his
bright colours stream across the canvas. Here from *My Sister
Life* is a poem written in farewell to a mistress:

AFTERWORD

No, it is not I who caused your grief,
It is not I who made you leave the country.
It was the sun aflame on drops of ink
As on clusters of dusty currants.

In the blood of my thoughts and my letters
Cochineal appeared.
That insect's purple was not of my making:
No, it is not I who caused your grief.

It was the evening cleaving to the dust, all ablaze
    with fire.
I kissed you, smothered by the yellow pollen,
While the shadows felt your pulse. By the fences
You walked, opening your face to the fields.
You were a flame swimming in the varnish of gates,
Drowned in twilight, poppies and ashes.

It was high summer glowing on the labels
Along the pools like luggage smeared by the sun,
Stamping the sailor's chest with scarlet wax,
And setting all your dresses and hats on fire.

It was your lashes glued against the bright sun—
The bestial sun whose horns are polished clear,
Butting over the fences and smashing the palisades.
It was the west, which flew into your hair,

A ruby buzzing for half an hour, then dying
Into the purple and scarlet of raspberries.
It was not I—it was your beauty!

It is a dangerous poem, very close to virtuosity, yet avoiding
it by a miracle. The images are continually changing: the sunset becomes a ruby, a bumblebee, a cluster of raspberries; hats
burst into flame; shadows feel pulses; and all of summer is contained on the sailor's chest. But how right it all is! How right
he is even when he sees the sunlit ink on the table, and reflects
that dusty currants shine with the same gleaming light when
the sun falls on them, and then reflects further that the ink and
the currants are images of his abandoned love affair, as valid
as Anna Akhmatova's mists and shadows, and perhaps more
valid because they are completely fresh and unexpected. In
his power to create new and unforgettable images Pasternak is
unrivalled, but his major achievement in poetry lay in another
direction altogether—in his power to sustain rich and varied
moods which had never been explored before.

In 1918, when Moscow was in the throes of typhus and everyone was starving, he wrote a poem which is an allegory of the
life of the poet. Simultaneously we see Elizabethan England and
Moscow under war-communism:

E

SHAKESPEARE

A coaching yard, and rising from the river
In terraces—the criminal and gloomy Tower:
Ringing hooves, and Westminster's chill bells,
And the headsman's block all draped for mourning.

The narrow streets, the drunken leaning walls
Hoarded the damp in all their branching timbers:
Morose from soot, and sodden as with beer,
Cold as all London, with teetering footfalls.

The snow fell sluggishly in lazy circles,
All the doors shuttered while it tumbled.
Like wrinkled crawling stomachers
It smothered all the sleepy vacant lots.

A tiny window with bits of leaded mica
Lilac-coloured. 'You can see by the weather
We'll soon be sleeping in the open air,
Or on a barrel, eh? Barber, bring water!'

As he shaves he holds his sides and cackles
At a clown's jests, unwearied by this feast,
Straining through a pipe-stem stuck to his lips
These tedious trifles.

                    Shakespeare no longer had
A taste for joking. Bored, he remembered
A sonnet composed in the night at white heat,
Not a blot anywhere, there on the far table
Where curdled rennet lapped at lobsters' claws.
The sonnet spoke aloud:

                    'I must admit,
You are extremely talented, most perfect master,
But do you know—you and that idiot there,
Striding a barrel with soap on his silly face—
I am the colour of lightning, I belong
To the utmost nobility—and you, sir,
Scorched by my flame, stink like your foul tobacco.'

'Father, forgive my—my filial scepticism,
But sir, my good lord, I believe we are
In an inn? Where's my place in your circle?
Your verses, for the filthy mob? Grant me the open
        spaces!'

'Then read to him! Why not, sir,
In the name of all guilds and bills,
Five yards away—you in the billiard room
Are you not content with your billiard room fame?'

'Read to him! You're mad!' He calls for the waiter,
And fiddling with a bunch of Malaga grapes
Reckons: half pint, French stew—and through the door
Hurls his napkin at the face of the apparition.

In this poem all virtuosity has been tossed overboard; it is London to the life, and Shakespeare to the life; we forget that Moscow and Pasternak are both implicated. But with what startling freshness he paints the familiar scene of the Mermaid Tavern! He is already the poet in full command of his medium, calm and passionate, detached and helplessly involved, never so certain of himself as when he finds himself describing emotions and ideas on the edge of thinking. Marianne Moore talks somewhere of real frogs in imaginary gardens. Pasternak has given us a real Shakespeare in a real London. It is a dazzling feat, and in later years, although the language became sparer and some of the youthful enthusiasm left him, he still wrote with the same precision, the same lucidity. Only the violence, smouldering beneath the clear-cut orderly lines, became greater.

FIVE

Four Short Stories

BETWEEN 1915 and 1923 Pasternak wrote four short stories covering altogether less than a hundred pages, which were to become remarkably famous. They were not short stories in the accepted sense of the term; they were completely unlike the stories of Chekhov or Tolstoy; and they did not set out to describe easily recognizable human situations. They were concerned with philosophical concepts, with the nature of the self and the nature of poetry and the nature of war. They were written in a close-knit and lapidary style, and they are the despair of his translators. Evidently they are stories written out of almost intolerable necessity. He wrote them by chipping them off his own breastbone, in despair and anguish, never knowing whether he could complete them or breathe sufficient life into them, and every one of the four stories remains uneven and fragmentary. Of the longest of the four stories Prince Mirsky wrote: 'Russian prose here reaches its greatest height.'

Much more, of course, than Russian prose is involved in the stories. Pasternak was concerned with forging a prose style, but he was also concerned to say things in prose which could not be said in poetry. Writing at a time of war and revolution, during a period when the full flood of his poetry was at its height, he was attempting to set down his most secret thoughts, his wildest desires, his deepest philosophical theories. These stories are weighted with significance. Pasternak makes no attempt to come to terms with the accepted method of telling stories: he tells them in his own way, in a startling mixture of fact and poetry. At any moment his stories will involve unexpected paradoxes and ambiguities, sleights of hand, sudden descents into the inferno and equally sudden ascents in the upper air. We never know, when the anchor is dropped, whether the ship will sink to the bottom of the sea or take flight with its sails outspread. There are passages of intensely wrought poetic prose followed by conversations which at first give an impression of pure banality, until we realize that he is saying by indirection things which can only be said in this way. The lover and the child speak on many levels, and Pasternak has attempted a prose which will reveal all these perceptible levels. His prose like his poetry is orchestrated, and does in fact give the impression of a full orchestra rather than a single musical instrument. This is prose where every single resource of poetry and music, of the clash of consonants and the singing of the vowels, is used to full capacity. To read him in Russian is to become aware of an extraordinary command of language.

It is precisely this lapidary and highly evolved use of language which presents difficulties to the Russian as well as the English reader. Nothing quite like this use of language had ever been known before. He will make ordinary words bear a weight almost beyond their powers. He will say things which one would have thought could not be said. At its best, his prose can be compared only with the great orchestrated passages of Sir Thomas Browne in *The Garden of Cyrus* and *Religio Medici* and the brilliant musical improvisations of the French poet Arthur Rimbaud.

Here for example is a passage from Rimbaud's recently discovered meditation on Jesus at the pool of Bethesda:

C'est là que Jésus fit la première action grave, avec les infâmes infirmes. Il y avait un jour, de février, mars ou avril, où le soleil de deux heures après-midi laissait s'étaler une grande faux de lumière sur l'eau ensevelie; et comme, là-bas, loin derrière les infirmes, j'aurais pu voir tout ce que ce rayon seul éveillait de bourgeons et de cristaux et de vers, dans ce reflet, pareil à un ange blanc couché sur le côté, tous les reflets infiniment pâles remuaient.

It was there that Jesus performed his first grave action with the terrible cripples. There was a day in February, March or April when the sun of two o'clock in the afternoon spread out a great sickle of light on the buried waters; and there, far beyond the cripples, I might have seen all that this single flash of light awakened among the budding flowers and crystals and worms, just as this beam, like an angel of perfect whiteness lying on her side, revealed all the infinitely pale reflections trembling.

Rimbaud is here describing a scene almost beyond description. It is the moment when the angel troubles the waters, when Jesus is about to heal the cripples assembled around the pool of Bethesda, which is covered with scum and yet glitters with the holy light of His presence. Rimbaud attempts to describe the exact moment of the theophany, the sudden descent of Power, by using words which shock and dazzle and resound against one another, reverberating along the entire length of the paragraph. The juxtapositions are deliberately frightening: the worms are given pride of place beside the white angel, who is perhaps only the pool seen in the light of another dispensation. He is using quite ordinary words— sickle, flash, budding flowers, crystals—but he is assembling them in an extraordinary way, producing the effect of a brilliant photomontage, so that we feel ourselves in the presence of the divinity and of the reeking cripples. There are sexual overtones to the passage, which moves with a relentless audacity and urgency. In a few luminous lines—it is remarkable how many of the words suggest gleams of splintering light—he has brought the reader to an afternoon in spring just outside the walls of Jerusalem where a vast miracle is being performed.

What Rimbaud was trying and largely succeeding in doing is perfectly legitimate. He is employing language to its utmost purposes. There is not one word or rhythm out of place. Every instrument in the orchestra is being used accurately and purposefully, with tremendous effect. Rimbaud conducts the orchestra with complete mastery, and the listener is entirely at his mercy.

Pasternak's techniques are very similar to Rimbaud's. There is the same ambiguity about time, the same delight in juxtaposing and comparing the incomparable, the same audacity in describing and enlarging on the indescribable. Like Rimbaud, Pasternak will invent exquisitely subtle musical rhythms and force his words into them. Emotion, vision—these are the

important things, and the words are merely slaves to do his
bidding.

There are, however, dangers in writing such highly wrought
prose. The temptation to produce virtuoso pieces must be
almost irresistible. But Pasternak was far too good a poet and
far too good a musician to permit himself the luxury of being
a virtuoso. From the beginning he wrote with tact and accuracy, and his earliest story, which foreshadows *Doctor
Zhivago*, is a nearly faultless example of his command over
the orchestra. It is also one of the most complex short stories
ever written, with so many levels of meaning that the dazed
reader may be excused if he hurries on to read the simpler
stories.

The Sign of Apelles

Pasternak's first published short story, written in 1915 while
he was working as a clerk in a chemical factory in the Urals,
describes the adventures of a young poet in search of his
identity. The theme of the story is given in the rubric, which
reads: *They say that when the Greek artist Apelles discovered that his
rival Zeuxis was not at home, he drew a line on the wall so that Zeuxis
would be able to guess who had come in his absence. Zeuxis did not
remain long in debt to his fellow artist. He chose a time when he knew
Apelles would be away, and he too left his mark—this line which became
the signature of all art.* Throughout, the story bears close to the
theme of the poet in search of his signature, his sign of Apelles,
and increasingly the reader becomes aware that everything in
the story is directly connected with the famous anecdote
concerning Apelles and Zeuxis, which he has annotated and
enlarged and explained very much as a Christian commentator
will annotate, enlarge and explain a brief text from the Bible.
The mysterious comings and goings of the protagonists reflect
the mysterious behaviour of Apelles and Zeuxis, whose signatures have the peculiar property of absence. For Pasternak, as
for Mallarmé, 'absence' is a passionate and positive thing,
almost a character in the story.

In Pasternak's version of the story Apelles assumes the form
of the Italian poet Emilio Relinquimini and Zeuxis is Heinrich
Heine, who is not the familiar Heine, but a young Russian

poet masquerading under this name. One evening Apelles–Relinquimini calls on Zeuxis–Heine in Pisa, and leaves his card:

> On one of those Septembery evenings when the leaning tower of Pisa leads a whole army of leaning sunsets and shadows against the city, when all Tuscany, irritated by the night wind, smells like a frayed laurel leaf held between the fingers, on such an evening—I remember the date very well, it was the 23rd August—Emilio Relinquimini, not finding Heine at the hotel, demanded paper and candle from an obsequiously fawning lackey. And when the lackey reappeared, bringing together with the objects which had been asked for an ink bottle, a pen holder, a seal and a stick of sealing wax, Relinquimini waved him away with a gesture of the utmost fastidiousness. Removing the pin from his tie, he held it over a candle and waited until it was white hot, then pricked himself in the finger, then snatching up one of the inn-keeper's cards, he bent down one corner with his bleeding finger. Then he handed the card nonchalantly to the lackey, saying: 'Give this to Herr Heine. Tomorrow I shall visit him at the same hour.'

It is a good beginning, but it is not Pasternak: it is a young poet writing his first short story and borrowing from the most likely source available. The style and mood are borrowed directly from Heinrich von Kleist, and especially from the opening paragraph of the scandalous short story called '*Die Marquise von O.*':

> In M., an important city in northern Italy, the widowed Marquise d'O., a lady of excellent reputation and the mother of several well-bred children, announced in the newspaper that for reasons unknown to her she found herself in an interesting condition, that the father of the child she was about to bear should present himself to her, and that she was resolved out of consideration for her family to marry him.

Having accomplished a triumphant *pastiche* of Heinrich von Kleist—to savour the full force of Pasternak's impropriety one should read the whole story—Pasternak immediately abandons his quarry and discovers his own voice. It is a voice reasonably familiar to readers of *Doctor Zhivago*, written more than thirty years later:

> The leaning tower of Pisa broke through the chain of medieval fortifications. The number of people who could see it from the bridge was increasing each moment. The red glow of the sunset crawled like a host of partisan fighters across the square. Tiptilted shadows blocked the streets, other shadows fought among themselves in the narrow alleyways. The tower of Pisa continued its headlong march, mowing everything down before it, until at last one insane gigantic shadow rose to hide the sun. The day ended.

The particular virtues of Pasternak's style are not yet fully apparent. We do not quite believe in this brief vision of Italy set against a background of embattled nature, and in fact the scenery in 'The Sign of Apelles' remains oddly Russian. But this is the first of a long series of set pieces, and among them are to be found some of the most gloriously evocative passages ever written.

As Pasternak tells the story, Relinquimini's bloodstained card is handed to Heine that evening. Heine accepts the card with enthusiasm, remembering that he received a few days before in Westphalia an utterly preposterous letter challenging him to establish his identity in the manner of Apelles. He realizes that the letter must have come from Relinquimini, the author of *Il Sangue* ('The Blood'). 'Love,' wrote the Italian poet, 'is the bloodstained cloud, which often wholly overlays our cloudless blood.' Such is his signature, or rather a hint of it. Heine prepares his own mysterious signature by cutting off a corner of one of his manuscripts; this torn fragment of manuscript reads: 'Rodolfina and Enrico have discarded their old names and changed them for names hitherto unprecedented, for he cried wildly: "Rodolfina", and she wept: "Enrico".'

At this point we need not concern ourselves with the working out of the story in great detail. Briefly: Heine on impulse takes a train to Ferrara, the native town of Relinquimini, and immediately gets in touch with the editor of *Il Voce* and inserts an advertisement in the newspaper describing how he found a lost manuscript belonging to Relinquimini in the train, and is prepared to surrender the manuscript to the rightful owner, who may claim it by calling at the Hotel Torquato Tasso. The owner arrives in the shape of the beautiful Camilla Ardenze, and Heine immediately falls in love with her. The greater part of the story describes the extraordinarily ribald and intricate tête-à-tête which follows their meeting, wandering from one hotel room to another and out into the square and back again to the hotel. They are duellists, fiercely determined to 'identify their signatures', and at the same time they are lovers, hopelessly entangled in one another. Pasternak is immensely taken by his young lovers, and paints them in the most seductive colours.

But before Heine takes the train to Ferrara, he decides to have one last look at Pisa at night, and this is what he sees:

On the paving stones, on the asphalt piazzas, along the balconies of Pisa and the embankments of the Arno, the people burned in the aromatic scent of a Tuscan night. Out of the blaze of darkness came a scent which lay heavy on the suffocating alley-ways and the dust-laden plane trees; and this burning, oily splendour was crowned with scattering sheaves of starlight and with clusters of prickly haze. These clusters of light overflowed the bowl of Italian patience; and from the heat of their fervour they uttered curses, as though they were prayers, and merely glancing at Cassiopeia they wiped the dusty sweat from their brows. Handkerchiefs gleamed in the dark like shaken thermometers, and the readings of these cambric thermometers spread perniciously along the streets, spreading the oppressive heat in the same way that eavesdropped rumours, epidemics and panic fear will spread it. And just as the leaning town disintegrated unconditionally, all the streets, the houses, and the courtyards, so in the same way the night air became compounded of separate and motionless collisions, ejaculations, bloody quarrels and encounters, whispers, laughter, voices silently dropping away. The echoes of these things existed as dust-laden and complex *interweavings*, and stood out in rows, arising from the pavement like trees, suffocating and colourless in the light of gas flares. Fantastically and powerfully the night of Pisa traced a limit to human endurance. Only a hand's breadth away chaos began.

Only a hand's breadth away chaos began. . . . It is the eternally recurring theme of Pasternak—the exploration of the frontiers, the sense of the encompassing dark, the knowledge of the wavering line between the shadowy earth and the heavenly light. What is remarkable about this passage is that here for the first time we hear his fully orchestrated voice in all its fullness and extraordinary complexity. There is no diffuseness. The images follow one another in their proper order, and each image is explored with a proper intensity. We know this particular night as we know nights we have lived through in strange countries, where everything surprises us, where we are borne along on a current of new and ever sharper sensations, without the blunting of the senses which comes from familiarity. Pasternak has the gift of being able to transform everything he sees until it glows with a fierce, incandescent light.

Light, indeed, is almost one of the characters of the story. Russian has dozens of compound words to suggest the various shades of blazing and glowing light, and Pasternak uses these words with amazing effect. He is perfectly aware that his characters may burst into flame at any moment. Here is Heine explaining himself to Camilla Ardenze, whose name is itself an indication of her incandescence:

Yes, of course, I am play-acting. Am I not allowed to stay for a while in the glare of the arc lamps? Am I at fault if the more dangerous places in life—bridges and crossroads —are illuminated more strongly than any others? How harsh is the light, and all the rest is submerged in darkness. On such a bridge—or stage—a man catches fire, he is lit by maddening flames, as if he were on show, ringed round with barriers, against the panorama of the city, precipices, the signal lights in the harbour.

In such passages—there are many others—Heine is asserting his right to penetrate the place of supreme danger, where the fire burns brightest. He is not play-acting any more than Hamlet is play-acting. He is saying in the simplest possible words that danger is his element, and it is perhaps not surprising that this German poet, ostensibly preparing to seduce an Italian poetess (for Camilla Ardenze is the disguise of Emilio Relinquimini), should find himself thinking of the harbour lights of Odessa. We should be prepared for such complexities when unravelling one of Pasternak's stories.

These complexities and obscurities are the price we pay for the enjoyment of the highest art. Pasternak is not obscure by design, but by necessity: he is trying to say things which have not been said before. For him words, and especially images, possess magical properties. Words change direction, gather speed, turn somersaults, disappear and spring up from a totally unexpected quarter, like rabbits from a conjurer's hat. To tame the words, to make sure he is understood, he will describe at length a very small incident in the story, while dismissing cavalierly an important development as almost unworthy of attention. These obscurities are not so much due to the suppression of links in the chain as to deliberate method. His task is to extract all the juice from the orange, to tell the story in all its ripeness. His technique resembles that of the Italian film makers who will suddenly and for no apparent reason (though the reason eventually becomes clear) drown their characters in a battery of arc lamps, with the effect of making them almost transparent.

Pasternak does exactly this when the time comes to describe Heine's overwhelming affection for the girl who has so wilfully fallen into his trap. Camilla is reduced to transparency, to the most perfect fluidity: she is a wave drowning in a wave:

> He observed to his unspeakable surprise that she was really beautiful, that she was beautiful to the extent of being completely unrecognizable, that the pulse of his heart throbbed like the sea under the stern sheets of a ship, a pulse which rose over knees drawing ever nearer, a pulse which poured over her in lazy waves, causing a trembling in her silken dress, calmly flooding her shoulders and lapping her chin, and—oh, miracle!—gently raising it a little, higher

and higher—the signora was now up to the throat in his heart: one wave more, and she will be drowning in it. Heine embraced the drowning woman—a kiss—a kiss which whirled them away out of the whirlpool, while he sighed under the pressure of their breaking hearts, twitched and tore himself upwards, forwards, devil knows in what direction; and she offered no resistance at all. On the contrary, she was borne away and wholly intimidated by kisses, singing, saying: 'I shall be a boat for your kisses. Only take me, take me.'

'Someone is knocking!' the words came with a hoarse sound from Camilla's throat. 'They're knocking!' And she tore herself from his embrace.

What has happened is the appearance of a *deus ex machina* in the shape of an enchanting ragamuffin in torn trousers, whose arrival signifies that the moment of illumination has come, or is about to come. The ragged boy occupies in the story the same role which is played by the mysterious half bother Evgraf in *Doctor Zhivago*, who appears at critical moments like an envoy of destiny, always present when news of shattering importance is announced or when there is a 'fatal intervention' in the progress of the doctor's life. Unlike Evgraf, the boy Giulio is incapable of menace, for he is Eros, his head hidden in the vast profusion of flowers which Heine has ordered, and the lower part of his body only too visible, for the trousers seemed to have been fashioned out of a conglomeration of fish nets. Heine decides to buy the trousers.

'Tell me, you little monkey, what do you think your trousers are worth?'

'Giulio is black and blue with scratches, Giulio is green with cold, Giulio has no other clothes, Giulio has neither father nor mother . . .' the ten-year-old ragamuffin whimpered sweatily. 'A hundred *soldi*, signor,' the boy said gently and dreamily. He looked like someone bewitched.

In fact all the characters of the story are bewitched: some are bewitched more than others. Heine is hopelessly bewitched; Camilla, the boy, the people in the hotel, and Ferrara itself are all bewitched, because they are all inextricably involved in discovering the sign of Apelles, which Heine describes very gravely in one of his conversations with Camilla when he says:

'You are able to look at things with such lively intelligence. Already you are master of the line, which is unique, like life itself. Only do not let it fall from your grasp. And do not throw the burden on me. Extend it as far as it will go. And then trace it still farther.'

In the end, as we might have expected, the sign of Apelles is the duty imposed upon the artist, and at the very end of his life Pasternak was speaking in the same terms, with the same gravity and the same determination to discover the laws of art. From the very beginning the moralist was present. He was saying that in a single line he must express all that was most vital in his art, and this was the simplest and the most inhumanly difficult thing of all.

Letters from Tula

For Pasternak there was to be no end to the search for the sign of Apelles. The quest, begun in his first story, was to be continued throughout his life, and long after he had finished *Doctor Zhivago*, he was still describing it in the close-knit poems written in his Olympian old age. What is a poet? What is his function in society? Why is he permitted to exist? How can he draw his indelible sign? Can he hope to be recognized, and can he recognize the signs of others?

'The Sign of Apelles' was an allegory; it was also a charming and ribald account of a young poet falling head over heels in love with a young woman, and painting his signature on her. 'Letters from Tula', written in 1918, the year of starvation and cholera and civil war, is altogether sterner stuff. It is almost a soliloquy. There is no attempt to be gay and amusing. The poet finds himself in Tula and grimly pursues his vocation, conscious of the shadow of Tolstoy which broods over the place, for Tula is only a few miles from Yasnaya Polyana, where Tolstoy wrote most of his works. The story consists of a number of unfinished letters from the poet to the mistress he has left behind in Moscow; there is a visit to a group of actors making a film dealing with medieval history; and then quite suddenly we are introduced to an old actor in his hotel bedroom, 'a man in ancient nankeens', who has watched the actors and is incapable of determining whether they had somehow entered the eighteenth century. The old man goes mad, and thinks he is himself acting on the stage, but there is no stage, only the silence and emptiness of the hotel room. Long after we have read the story we realize that the poet and the old actor are the same person. The story, which covers only ten pages, ends with the poet returning by train to Moscow. In a sense there is no story, only a series of impressions linked together by mood and atmosphere and a strange sense of urgency.

Though 'Letters from Tula' succeeds brilliantly as an improvisation in a new form, it is chiefly remarkable for the poet's letters which are concerned with the nature of poetry and the poet's existence. He writes:

> O grief and longing! I beat back and blunt my furious frustration with verses!

> How mischievous it is to be born a poet! How the imagination tortures you! The sun—in beer. It sinks to the very depths of the bottle. Opposite me at my table there is a farm bailiff, or something of the sort. Ruddy-faced. He stirs the coffee with green fingers. Ah, my dear, they are all strangers here. There was one witness (the general), but he went away. There is still another—the magistrate—they won't recognize me. Oh, nonentities! They think they can lap up the sunshine with milk from a saucer. They do not realize that in your, in our sun their flies get stuck, the cook's saucepans clash together, the seltzer water splutters noisily and rubles tinkle sonorously on the marble table top, like a smacking noise with the tongue. . . .
> Alas, to write is only to torture oneself. But I have not the strength to stop.

So he goes on in those amazing letters, describing the world of the frontier, which is also the world of the poet, driven half to madness by the vulgarity of the actors, while the noises of the encroaching railway punctuate the writer's thoughts. We see Pasternak in the process of hammering out his own style, obsessed, as always, with the claims of a pervasive morality, seeing the world around him by the light of an incandescent core of morality. One of these brief letters, which contains an invocation to conscience, became deservedly famous.

2 o'clock

I swear to you that the faith of my heart is greater than it ever was, the time will come—no, let me tell you about it later. O night, tear me to pieces, torment me, burn me to ashes: may the forgotten, the furious word *conscience* blaze with a fiery flame. [A stroke under the word 'conscience' has ripped through the page.] O maddening flame of burning oils, illuminate the floor of the night!

There has come into existence a certain way of regarding life, and as a result there is no place on earth where a man can warm his soul with the fire of shame. Shame is everywhere watered down and cannot burn. Falsehood and confused dissipation. Thus for thirty years all who were gifted, young and old, have been damping down their shame, and now at last it has spread to the whole universe, even to the unknown places. For the first time, for the first time since the days of childhood I am being consumed by flames. [This whole sentence crossed out.]

One more attempt. The letter was not posted.

How shall I describe it to you? I must begin from the end. Or else I shall never write it at all. And now permit me to talk in the third person. Wasn't I writing about the man who was walking past the luggage office? Well, the poet—from now on we shall put the word, until he is cleansed by fire, in inverted commas—the 'poet' sees himself in the unseemly behaviour of the actors and in the outrageous spectacle which points a finger of accusation at his friends and at his generation. Perhaps he is only playing with the idea. No. They confirm him in the belief that his identity is in no way chimerical. They rise and move toward him. 'Colleague,' they say, 'could you kindly give us change for

three rubles?' He dispels the illusion. It isn't only actors
who shave. 'Here are twenty kopecks for three rubles.'
So he gets rid of the actors. Obviously the affair doesn't
depend on being shaved or not.

What Pasternak is saying here is that the affair is amazingly
complex, depending upon forces over which the poet has
pathetically little control, so that one can almost define the
poet's identity as the sum total of all the uncontrollable forces
that move him; and the most uncontrollable of all—and in
Pasternak's vision the most daemonic and terrifying—is the
sense of place, the knowledge of all the countless actions which
have taken place at the crossroads of the world, the mysterious
quality which places assume when legends are attached to
them.

For all the Russians, and especially for Pasternak, the railway station at Tula was a place of legend, haunted by the
presence of Tolstoy. How many times the old master had
taken the train there! 'No wonder the magnetic needles begin
to dance here!' Pasternak writes. 'Everything that happens
happens from the nature of the place. This is an event in the
realm of *conscience*.'

Almost Pasternak is inclined to attribute superhuman powers
to railway stations, and the finest passages of 'Letters from
Tula' are devoted to a meditation of the poet as he patrols the
deserted platform at night. Out of the leaping darkness strange
signals flash, smoke and steam rise unaccountably, and furious
beasts fashioned out of hammered iron thunder past the platform; when the engine-driver pulls the string of the whistle,
there is a sound like a vast and echoing cockcrow. From his
point of isolation in the waiting-room the poet sees himself
in the presence of the generative womb of the night; nothing
more like the act of creation is conceivable.

To enforce this vision, to give it depth and sonority, Pasternak deliberately introduces the parallel story of the old
actor alone in his cheap hotel room, communing with his
fears—with loneliness, madness and old age. The actor acts
out his own drama and pursues his own meditations while the
poet meditates in the railway station. For him, too, time has

F

vanished. He has watched the film actors clawing their way up the cliffs, doing battle with painted swords and axes— 'those axes which were insensible to sunlight and curiously soundless'—and in despair he set himself to seek through all the fragments of his remembered repertoire in order to discover some clue to the event. But there are no clues. A legend is being invented, but it corresponds to nothing he knows. He recites some lines of doggerel, watches the solitary lamp burning in the window—that lamp intended to guide some woman out of his past who will one day come back to him— and then it comes to him that he has reached the hour of his death:

He sat by the table, held his head in his hands, and sank into deep thought. He came to the conclusion that this was his death. This inward struggle bore no resemblance to his past years, which were unwaveringly bitter. He decided to take the medals from the cupboard and to warn someone, the doorkeeper—no matter whom—and meanwhile he went on sitting there, hoping that it was nothing and would pass away.

The horse tram tinkled as it passed. It was the last tram going to the station.

Half an hour passed. A star gleamed. Otherwise there was not a soul in sight. A candle was burning, trembling. The soft silhouette of a bookcase, composed of four dark and flowing lines, rose in waves. Meanwhile the night uttered a long-drawn throaty sound. Far away. In the street a door banged, and people began talking agitatedly, in voices becoming to the spring evening, no one about, only a light in the room upstairs, and the window opening. . . .

He had reached the end, and he now saw both of them— himself and the young woman. Noiseless sobbing choked him. Hours passed. He wept and made whimpering sounds. There followed an extraordinary silence. And while the old man shuddered and helplessly dabbed his face and eyes with a handkerchief, and trembled and crumpled it, shaking his head and beating the air with his hands, like someone giggling, like someone who had suffocated and was sur-

prised because, God forgive him, he was still whole and
the experience had not shattered him—at this very moment
they began to couple the carriages for Eletz.

To the reader of *Doctor Zhivago*, these letters from Tula are
oddly disturbing with their portraits of a young poet weighed
down with conscience and an old man suffocating to death in
sight of the passing trams. In the end Pasternak combined
these portraits, rounded them out, gave weight and significance
to the preliminary sketch, and from these small beginnings he
produced a masterpiece. Nearly all of *Doctor Zhivago* is contained in embryo in this short, closely written sketch.

The Childhood of Luvers

Just as the future Doctor Zhivago makes his first appearance in 'Letters from Tula', so the beautiful and enigmatic
Larissa appears for the first time in 'The Childhood of Luvers',
the most perfectly accomplished of all Pasternak's short stories.
This, too, was written in 1918, the year of plagues and wars,
but the story is concerned with the evocation of a peaceful
childhood in another age. It is Pasternak's quiet protest against
the absurdity of the time he was living in.

With this story Pasternak comes at last to full command of
his medium. There is no effort to impose his own voice; the
language is rich and orchestrated, but it is the language of a
young girl who is overwhelmed by wonder at the world, yet
she remains a sensible person, and she knows she will survive,
even beyond those frontiers where chaos begins. Though she
inhabits a world where the shaggy bearskins, chairs and stupid
governesses are unquestionably real, she knows that the real
world sometimes vanishes to give place to the troubling appearance of divine mysteries. She is perfectly at home among
these mysteries which her parents have long forgotten and
perhaps never known.

The portrait of Zhenia Luvers[1] is a quite extraordinary
accomplishment: no one who has watched her growing up has

[1] Luvers is a fairly common name around Liège in Belgium. A surprising
number of Belgian engineers were working in the Urals before the war.
Zhenia and Larissa in *Doctor Zhivago* are both partly Belgian.

ever been able to forget her. It is a portrait in depth, in blazing colours, with the lens opening so wide on the heroine that we seem to absorb her and become part of her without quite knowing how the miracle is accomplished. She is more living than any of Pasternak's creations. She is even more living than the majestic Larissa, who is Zhenia after she has been refined and tamed by experience. Yet they are demonstrably the same person, quick, beautiful, ingenuous, wholly feminine. In the story her adventures are those of youth, natural in the sense that they are close to nature; in the novel she is at the height of her maturity, with no childishness in her. Quite deliberately in *Doctor Zhivago* he presented her as a woman of exquisite sensibility while possessing an almost godlike calm. But there is not the least suggestion of calm in the thirteen-year-old Zhenia whose sudden awakening into awareness on a night of happy delirium is recorded in the opening passages of the story:

Zhenia Luvers was born and raised in Perm, in a house full of shaggy bearskins. And just as her small boats and dolls were seeped in the smell of furs, so too in later years were her memories. Her father was the manager of the Luniev iron mines and had a wide clientèle among the mill owners of Chusovaya.

These furs were presents, luxurious, and of a dark russet colour. The white she-bear in Zhenia's room resembled an enormous crumbling chrysanthemum. This was the fur especially acquired for her room, chosen after long bargaining in the shop, and sent along by messenger.

In summer they lived in a country house on the banks of the Kama River. During those years they always insisted on sending her to bed early. She could not see the lights of Motovilikha. But once the Angora cat, startled by something or other, suddenly stirred out of its sleep and startled her awake. Then she saw grown-ups on the balcony. The alder tree, hanging over the railings, was thick and iridescent like ink. The tea in the glasses was bright red. Cuffs and cards—yellow. Tablecloth—green. It was like a delirium,

but it was a delirium which possessed a recognizable name—
they were playing cards.

On the other hand it was absolutely impossible to deter-
mine what was happening on the other side of the river far,
far away. It had no name, no sharp contours, no recognizable
colour; and when it became excited, it was familiar and dear
to her, and was not at all a delirium, not at all like the
rumbling and rolling of clouds of tobacco smoke which
threw fresh and wind-swept shadows on the chestnut-
coloured beams of the gallery. Zhenia burst into tears. Her
father came in and explained what had happened. The
English governess turned her face to the wall. It was—Motovilikha. Shameful. Such a big girl. Go to sleep. But Zhenia
understood nothing and contentedly swallowed a falling tear.
There was only one thing she wanted: to unravel the name
of the unknowable—Motovilikha. That night everything
could still be explained, for that night the name still possessed
a full and reassuring childish significance.

But when morning came, she began to ask questions about
what was Motovilikha and what happened there at night,
and she was told that Motovilikha was a government factory
where pig iron was made, and out of pig iron . . . but all this
no longer amused her, and what she wanted to know was
whether there were certain countries called 'factories', and
who lived there; but she did not ask these questions and for
some reason deliberately concealed them.

That morning she emerged from her childhood. . . .

Such is the deservedly famous hallucinatory beginning of
'The Childhood of Luvers', which brings the reader in a single
bound into the heart and mind of a young girl. It is, of course,
a poet's prose; it sings, and carries the reader along on the
strength of its voice. Like all good poetry it appears to be
artless, but is in fact highly contrived, fitted together sentence
by sentence like polished blocks of marble. To accomplish his
purpose, to bring the reader in a minimum of time into the
presence of Zhenia, Pasternak has employed a multitude of
artifices, beginning with the most obvious indications of place
and time and deliberately interweaving them into the flow

of her thoughts and the blinding discovery of her own awareness of the outside world. He never describes her; we never
know what face she shows to the world; but we come to know
what face the world showed to her. From childhood she flows
like quicksilver into adolescence.

At first reading 'The Childhood of Luvers' gives the effect of
a prodigious conjuring trick. Silk hats and ribbons appear
from nowhere; the silver chafing dishes, known to be empty,
contain snow-white pigeons. The normal resistance of words
is here triumphantly overcome. He will not permit words to
master him, but on the contrary he enslaves them, devours
them, crushes them underfoot, and when they are completely
at his mercy he compassionately breathes life into them. This
miracle is accomplished by the invention of long complex
sentences which delicately outline the thoughts of the growing girl and by the employment of images which soar like
skyrockets to illuminate the dark places of her mind.

Pasternak's technique is familiar to film makers—the close
shot, the middle shot, the long shot. The close shot is provided by the white she-bear which resembled 'an enormous
crumbling chrysanthemum'. The she-bear is not placed at
the beginning of the story fortuitously; it provides a precise
portrait of childhood crumbling away. The middle shot is
provided by the alder tree 'thick and iridescent like ink', and
the table covered with green baize with the card-players sitting
around it. The long shot is given by the fires pouring from the
smoke stacks of Motovilikha—that mysterious place, as
legendary as any enchanted city in a fairy tale, which becomes
the focus of her white-hot imagination. By night the place
exerts its magic; by morning all the magic will have gone, and
Zhenia will have entered the world of grown-ups and had her
first glimpse of that terrible world where 'everything is as it is'.
'The Childhood of Luvers' is the chronicle of Zhenia's exploration of the unpredictable world of grown-ups.

Into the young girl's mind facts come streaming in with the
effect of explosions. One morning she awakes to discover
blood on her nightgown and on the bed sheets. There is no
explanation for it. It has appeared by miracle, and must be
removed quickly in case it should ever happen again. Zhenia

decides to cut away the offending bloodstains with scissors, but a moment later it occurs to her there is a far better solution. She sprinkles the stains with the face powder of her French governess, who catches her in the act, imagines she is powdering her face, and slaps her. Filled with an obscure sense of shame, Zhenia retreats into herself, into the silent world of doubt and self-recrimination and horror, deciding not to throw herself into the Kama River 'because it was still cold and the last ice floes were floating down the river'.

That day, one of the longest days in her life, to be remembered as a day of guilt and quiet torment, coincides with the coming of spring. Pasternak describes the coming of spring as seen by the young girl trembling with her own expectancy:

> Outside it was spring. Spring in the Urals, so sickly, coming to maturity with so much difficulty, then furiously breaking loose in the course of a single night, only to continue in spate, stridently and tempestuously. The lamps with their shadows only stressed the emptiness of the evening air. They gave no light, but swelled from within like sick fruit, suffering from a clear and cloudy dropsy, which swelled the bloated lamp globes. They were absent. They were in fact in their proper places, exactly where they were needed, on the tables, and they descended from the sculptured ceilings of the rooms where she was accustomed to seeing them. Between the lamps and the room there were fewer points of contact than with the spring sky: the lamps in relation to the sky were like glasses of water brought to the bedside of a sick man. Zhenia's soul was wandering in the street, where the gossip of servant girls crawled along the damp earth, and the thin drip of their voices turned into ice with the coming of the night.

In Pasternak's poems and in *Doctor Zhivago* there are many descriptions of spring. For him it is always a visitation, a divine flowering, but the profound joy is always accompanied by an overwhelming melancholy. 'There is no grief,' he wrote in one of his poems, 'which cannot be cured by the winter snows.' But the griefs of spring are incurable, taking a man by the throat and removing him overnight out of the calm of winter into a delirium of the senses. Spring for the Russians is always an intoxication, followed by a hangover. It is a time of strange alterations of blood, of sudden unappeasable desires. The ice melts, the rain falls in torrents, the earth quickens. All creation is in a state of frenzy. Only Zhenia remains calm, absorbed in herself, absorbed in the careful wide-eyed contemplation of the universe unfolding around her.

She is not always calm. In the course of that long year there are moments when she surrenders to ferocious excitement. These moments are often inexplicable. The sight of a man limping, or of children in a neighbouring yard, or of some alteration in the colour of the sky will send her spirit reeling. One evening she decides to stay up late with a lamp and a copy of *The Fables of Kot-Murlika*, 'which is not for children'. She sucks chocolate and listens to the wind, while the snow falls. She is still reading contentedly when she glances up at the window and sees entire kingdoms whirling past her:

> The snowstorm was increasing. The sky quivered and white kingdoms and countries toppled from the sky, impossible to keep score of them, mysterious and terrible. It was obvious that these territories, falling from no one knew where, had never heard about life and the earth. Arctic and blind, they smothered the earth, neither seeing it nor knowing anything about it.
>
> They were exquisitely terrifying, these kingdoms: ravishingly satanic. Zhenia revelled as she gazed at them. The air staggered, grasping at this falling universe, and far, far away in great pain the whole countryside howled as though struck by lashes. Everything became confused. Night rushed upon them, maddened by that single grey thread which had fallen to the earth, cutting and blinding it. Everything was scattered, with a scream, taking no notice of the road. A shout and an echo disappeared, having never met: a confusion of sounds borne upward over many rooftops. Snowstorm.

Removed from its context, such passages give the impression of set pieces. With a phenomenal vocabulary, employing all the artifices of grammar, Pasternak concentrates all his poetic

gifts in depicting the violence of the storm; and in fact he is
writing a kind of prose which is very close to poetry. 'A good
prose sentence', wrote Flaubert, 'should be like a good line of
poetry—unchangeable, just as rhythmic, just as sonorous.'
But although Zhenia's vision of the white kingdoms sailing
past her window is among the most memorable things written
by Pasternak, it is perfectly integrated in the story. We are
inside the mind of Zhenia, and we are never allowed to emerge
from it. Every sentence, every word, is designed to keep us
within the burning core of her brain.

What is astonishing above everything else is Pasternak's
sure-footedness as he walks in dangerous regions. He describes
things which one would have thought beyond the powers of
anyone to describe. There are entire areas of human consciousness which he seems to have been the first to explore.
With exquisite tact and delicacy he will describe the colours
of the sky or the colours of the human soul; he will invent
atmospheres for them to bathe in; and he pours life into them.
There is never a moment when the attention is allowed to
stray. He watches closely, determined to extract significance
from every thing he sees. There are no still lives; everything
is in movement.

'The Childhood of Luvers' is almost an anthology of
famous passages. Among the most famous is the description of
Zhenia recovering from an attack of fever, which should be
quoted at length because it demonstrates his extraordinary
power to suggest the most intricate workings of a child's mind:

> It derived probably from someone's heavy footsteps out-
> side the door. The tea in the glass, on the little table by the
> bed, rose and fell. The slice of lemon in the tea rose and fell.
> The sunny stripes on the wallpaper were swaying. They
> were swaying like columns, like the bottles full of syrup in
> the shops behind signboards, on which a Turk is smoking a
> pipe.
> On which a Turk . . . is smoking . . . a pipe. Smoking . . .
> a pipe.
> It derived probably from someone's footsteps. The patient
> fell asleep again. . . .

For a fortnight she lay in a fever, her sweat thickly pow-
dered with painful red peppers which burned her and clung
to her eyelids and the corners of her lips. Perspiration tormented her, and a sensation of monstrous obesity mingled
with the feeling of being stung. As though the flame which
made her swell was being poured into her by a summer wasp.
As though its sting, as thin as a grey hair, remained in her
while she longed to take it out, more than once and in more
than one way. Now from the purple cheekbone, now from
the inflamed shoulder aching under her nightgown, now
from somewhere else. Meanwhile she was convalescing. The
feeling of weakness was everywhere.

This feeling of weakness gave way, at its own risk and
peril, to a strange geometry *entirely its own*. It provoked a
slight giddiness and nausea.

For example, beginning with an episode on the counter-
pane, this feeling of weakness began to construct on it rows
of gradually increasing blank spaces, which quickly became
an immense void when the impetuous rush of twilight assumed the shape of a public square which was the very basis
of that vagary of space. Or else, starting out from the pattern
of the wallpaper, it drove these stripes toward her, gliding as
smoothly as though they had been oiled, substituting one for
another, and also, as in all these sensations, harassing her with
their regular and steady growth in size. Or else it tortured
the sick child with depths which went on without end, betraying from the very beginning, from its first trick on the
parquet floor, its own fathomlessness, allowing the bed to fall
silently into the depths, silently; and with the bed went the
girl. Then her head would be in the position of a lump of
sugar thrown into the abyss of an insipid and menacingly
empty chaos, and it dissolved and disappeared in it.

This came about through the heightened sensitivity of
the labyrinths of her ears.

It derived from someone's footsteps. The lemon rose and
fell. The sunlight rose and fell on the wallpaper. Her mother
came in and congratulated her on her recovery, and produced on the girl the impression of someone able to read the
thoughts of others. While waking up, she had already heard

something similar. These were the congratulations of her own hands, feet, elbows, knees; and she accepted these congratulations as she stretched herself. These greetings had indeed wakened her up. And there was her mother as well. What a strange coincidence!

Pasternak writes of Zhenia's sickness with extraordinary authority, without supplying a single medical detail, with no other weapon than his overwhelming sympathy for her, and without apparent effort. Hallucination and incantation play their part. 'The lemon rose and fell. The sunlight rose and fell.' The mysterious Turk smoking his pipe plays perhaps the dominant role, for he casts a long spell on the entire scene. But it is in the precise working out of the details of Zhenia's vision of fever that Pasternak shows his consummate skill. The reader is not hovering over her; he is inside her, watching the fever.

Again and again Pasternak demonstrates a breath-taking power to enter into moods, feelings, atmospheres, by means of sudden assaults. There are moments of dusk and dawn, of sunlight and shadow and penumbra, which he alone seems to have understood and put down on paper. He resembles a perpetual barometer recording the delicate changes in the weather of the soul. Nearly all his descriptions of nature—and his work is filled with them—are designed to give depth and resonance to his characters. Nature is the robe they wear; a robe which does not conceal them, but reveals them completely.

Sometimes he will use the simplest and most audacious means to suggest a mood. 'The clouds were dirty and tattered, like sleigh rugs rubbed smooth with age. The day butted the window-pane with its snout, like a calf in its steaming stall. Why was it not spring?' So he writes in one of the concluding chapters of 'The Childhood of Luvers', and the mind reels at the quick changes of metaphor. Yet how wonderfully he has described a particular kind of wet and misty day, with what consummate artistry he has forced us to visualize the scene! The sleigh rug, the window-pane, the calf in the steaming stall, are magically fused together to convey a precise atmosphere, a particular colour of the air. It is Shakespeare's trick of piling

metaphor on metaphor, each one more startling than the other.
Or take his description of harbour lights at night:

> Far in the distance there was something mysterious and
> dark. Beyond the dockside warehouses were lights which the
> town rinsed in water, and they dangled from the shore and
> from ships. Then many more appeared, swarming in black
> clusters, greasily, blind like maggots. On Lyubimovsky wharf
> the funnels, the roofs of the warehouses and the decks were
> a sombre blue. Barges stared at the stars.

Once again the unexpected verb is followed by the unexpected
image. 'Rinsed' shocks us, and the lights 'swarming in black
clusters, greasily, blind like maggots' shocks us more. We
detect a kind of formula, for 'rinsed' corresponds to 'butts'
and 'maggots' to 'the calf in the steaming stall'. But life flows
through these brilliant improvisations, and though the formula
can be traced throughout his work, he employs it so variously
and with such accuracy that we are never offended. Only a
great poet can dare to fashion such outrageous metaphors.

When he is in full flight Pasternak will fling down one
metaphor after another; the fireworks explode in all directions,
but the pyrotechnic display possesses its own inner logic. The
train winds among hazel trees, and suddenly Zhenia sees the
Urals for the first time. It is a moment of epiphany. Nothing
so beautiful had ever appeared to her before:

> What she saw was beyond description. A forest of clam-
> orous hazel trees, into which they were poured by the ser-
> pentine train, became the ocean, became the world, became
> anything you pleased, everything. The forest ran on, bril-
> liantly clear, murmuring on its way down, very broad and
> steeply sloping, until, growing smaller, curdled and misty, it
> fell cleanly away, almost entirely black. And then there arose
> on the other side of the abyss an enormous and wonderful
> thundercloud, all green and white, full of whorls and curli-
> cues, plunged in thought and stupefied by torpor. Zhenia
> held her breath, and at once perceived the speed of that
> boundless and carefree air, and it occurred to her that the
> thundercloud was some country, some place bearing a

sonorous and mountainous name reverberating all round it with rocks and sand tumbling into the valley below; and the hazel trees did nothing but whisper it and whisper it: here, there, and away over there: nothing else.

'Is it the Urals?' she asked of the whole compartment, leaning forward.

Confronted with the Urals for the first time, Zhenia clings to the window in an ecstasy of delight. The train curls around them 'in a slow revolution, like the rotation of stars, with the prudent caution of giants anxious for the preservation of the earth, on the edge of catastrophe'. And this dizzy and terrifying vision pours into her, fills her whole body, changes her; and Pasternak produces this effect simply, almost without effort.

Zhenia's journey through the Urals is of course Pasternak's own journey. He was always writing about these mountains, which never failed to startle and delight him. He wrote about them first in 1915 in his collection of poems called *Over the Barriers*:

THE URALS FOR THE FIRST TIME

In darkness, no accoucheuse helping them,
The Urals pushed their hands against the night,
Half dead with agony, shrieking
In mindless pain against the birth of morning.

Toppled by chance, the highest mountains bled
Bronze boulders in thunderous volleys:
The train choked; and the ghostly fir trees
Swerved and shied at the piercing screams.

This smoky dawn flowered with opium
Fed from the mouths of flaming dragons:
So will a traveller on a journey
Feed opiates secretly to his fellow passengers.

Dawn was a flame. The poppy-coloured skies
Licked the foothills, hunters upon skis:
And the strangers came to kiss the forest's feet,
And on the firs they set the silver crowns.

> Arrayed in majesty, the firs arose
> In ranks of glory, and so they trod
> The orange velvet of the carpeted snows,
> The tinselled silk, the rich embroidered cloth.

It is a dazzling performance, but no more dazzling than many similar poems describing journeys. Trains are always appearing in his work; they are palpably godlike, dangerous, wildly exciting. For him they live and breathe, and he could no more regard them as lumps of metal than he could regard a flower as insentient. Asked once why he was always describing train journeys, Pasternak answered: 'Where else can you enjoy the supernatural? You go to the ticket office, pay some money, and you are transported to Paradise.' He enjoyed all train journeys, even journeys across the endless plains. He refused to travel by air, saying that the supreme advantage of the train was that it brought you closer to the earth.

Yet he did write one story about journeys through the air. It was called 'Aerial Ways', and was concerned with the mysterious roads in the air on which ideas and influences travel, and nothing he ever wrote was so hard, so close-packed, as this story which seems to have been written against the grain, hopelessly, in a moment of fear.

Aerial Ways

It was the year of the death of Lenin, with misery and hunger still knocking at the doors. It was the year of poverty, and the birth of his first child, Evgeniy, and of many poems about a marriage which had lost all meaning. No one knew or guessed that in the following year, 1925, the people of Moscow would 'begin to eat cake'.

Pasternak's story reflects the despair of the times. It is in fact five separate fragments of despair, only remotely connected with one another. Where 'The Childhood of Luvers' tells a consecutive story through a series of incidents clearly described, developing in full view of the reader, coming to a climax on the day when Zhenia becomes aware for the first time of the tragedy of life, 'Aerial Ways' goes beyond tragedy altogether and refuses to obey any laws whatsoever except the anarchic laws of its own fashioning. It is not so much a story as the recital of a walk through Hell.

As we might expect, Hell is inhabited by the Furies. These Furies assume the form of a sleeping nurse and a hare-lipped cow girl screaming at the top of her voice:

> The nurse slept under the age-old mulberry-tree, propped up against the trunk. When the enormous lilac-coloured cloud appeared at the end of the road, silencing even the grasshoppers chirping sultrily in the grass, and when the drums in the camp sighed and died away, then the eyes of the earth grew dark and there was no more life in the world.
>
> 'Whoa, there! Whoa!' cried the half-witted cow girl to the whole world, speaking through her harelips, and she kept dragging her crushed foot in front of the steer and brandishing a wild branch like a lightning flash, coming out of the cloud of rubbish from the far side of the orchard, where the thickets began: deadly nightshade, bricks, twisted wire and evil-smelling darkness.
>
> Then she vanished.

We never see the nurse or the cow girl again, nor do we need to see them. They have set the mood. We have come to the menacing landscape at the world's end, where nothing grows except the deadly nightshade. Obscurely through the murk we see a child wandering, and suddenly a black-bearded man with silver earrings, wearing a green caftan, pounces on it. Because a nurse has slept, because the Furies are abroad, the lost child is lost forever.

All that night the midshipmen at the local naval station search for the child along the cliffs, for the child's father is a midshipman. The mother, Lelia, is almost insane with grief. The father and mother look at the empty cot, and the sight of it 'strips the skin from their voices'. The midshipmen find no trace of the child. They wander in a landscape of pure horror, where 'the fields are churned and whipped by the wind, darkness and fear, as though by a black comb with three broken teeth'. They never find the child, which vanished like a stone in the sea.

The child was lost in 1905, the year of the abortive revolution.

Fifteen years pass. The midshipman becomes a communist, a local leader in the Red Army fighting in the Civil War, no longer interested in the wife who gave him two more children, for both of them died. He is the dedicated revolutionary, who believes that a new sky has dawned.

What had happened to the sky? Even during the day it suggested the image of night as seen in our youth and when we are on a journey. Even during the day it caught the eyes, infinitely remarkable. Even during the day it was saturated with the desolation of the earth, and it struck down the somnolent and raised the dreamers to their feet.

There were aerial ways. And on these roads, like trains, every day there flew the direct thoughts of a Liebknecht, a Lenin, and other similar minds. These roads had been established in a way which enabled them to pass over any frontier, whatever its name. One of these roads, opened during the war, preserved its previous strategical height imposed on it by the engineers, following the nature of the frontier over which they built it. It was an old military road, and cut the frontiers of Poland and then of Germany at a time and place of its own choosing—here, at the very beginning, before the eyes of everyone, avoiding the necessity of understanding mediocrity and of enduring it. It passed precisely over this courtyard, which feared the immense distances it was destined to reach and also its oppressive clumsiness, for the same reason that a fugitive suburb will fear a railway which gives it a wide berth.

Until he came to write *Doctor Zhivago*, Pasternak never permitted himself direct comments on the nature of communism; and this paragraph, with its intricate pleading and complicated syntax, is the only exception. The passage is richly poetic, darkly menacing, full of a curious quivering exaltation and anger. What is especially remarkable is the subdued, deliberate way in which Pasternak fills out the metaphor of 'the aerial ways', the roads in the sky through which all ideas travel.

Here and there, always fleetingly, Pasternak has spoken of communism in his poems. In 'The High Malady' he drew a heroic portrait of a legendary Lenin, and he lavished great care on the still more legendary Lieutenant Schmidt. But he had never wrestled with communism, never attempted to wrest its secrets. Here for the first time he spoke of the workings of communism, and characteristically he gave a special place to its enormous daring and 'oppressive clumsiness'. He was to speak of this clumsiness at greater length in *Doctor Zhivago*.

After the digressions, evasions and hesitations of the first part of the story, the last pages come as a relief. The midshipman turned communist leader comes into full focus. His headquarters are somewhere near the front. Not long before, there was a battle, and a certain Neploshayev has been captured, and will shortly be executed. That night a woman comes to his headquarters to intercede for her son, lost so many years ago, and then mysteriously found. 'It is Anton— our son,' she says, and so it is. The boy had entered military school, fought against the Bolsheviks, and for some reason assumed the name of one of his friends. The communist knows that nothing can be done to save the boy:

> He stood by the table and called another office on the telephone, and made certain inquiries, and moving now from one conversation to another he fell deeper and deeper into the town and into the night, until the abyss of the last and ultimate truth lay revealed before him.
>
> He looked around the room. He felt as though he had received a terrible blow between the eyes, and when he looked around the room it swam before him like stalactites, like rivers. He made to pluck the skin over the bridge of his nose, but instead he put his hand to his eyes, and the stalactites began to dance and stream in all directions. It would have been easier for him if these spasms had been less frequent, and not so silent. At last he found her. Like an enormous, unbroken doll she lay between the table and the chair, in the very same layer of sawdust and dirt which in the darkness and when she was still conscious, she had taken for the carpet.

So the story ends, as it began, in pain and horror: we are back again in the landscape of deadly nightshade, bricks,

G

twisted wire and evil-smelling darkness. The communist leader, called Lyov Polivanov in the story, will become Pasha Strelnikov in *Doctor Zhivago*. Lelia will become Larissa, the infinitely gentle and understanding heroine of the novel. Even Anton has his place in the novel, for he becomes the schoolboy Terenty Galuzin, who with twenty others was led to an open grave and shot by the partisans. Lightly wounded, covered by the bodies of the others, he somehow succeeded in crawling away and hiding in the forests. 'The only good thing about him,' says Strelnikov, 'is that he was devoted to his mother.' Terenty Galuzin plays a sinister role in the novel, betraying Strelnikov and being largely responsible for his death.

These four stories deserve to be read carefully, for they represent Pasternak at his most searching, at his most adventurous. Each story involves the hammering out of a new style, a new way of looking at the world. Significantly, when the stories were collected together, Pasternak called them after the story he liked best, 'Aerial Ways'. It is not perhaps the most enduring of the stories—'The Childhood of Luvers' has become a classic, and the other stories are rarely mentioned in the same breath—but it is the one which most clearly describes Pasternak's relationship to the communists. Lyov Polivanov, the man in the short unbuttoned jacket, seen in the light of a glimmering oil lamp, is an unforgettable and portentous figure: a terrifying ink blot obscuring the light of the sun.

So it is in all these stories, where Pasternak demonstrates an amazing power of concentration, of concentrated imagery. The particular virtues which are displayed in *Doctor Zhivago* are already present, but in a more emphatic form. Here, too, is to be found Pasternak's predilection for describing what can only be called the daemonic forces of nature, those hours when the heavens let loose their splendours: hours of stark sunset, of brooding dawns and fiery snowstorms, when ordinary mortals, accustomed to living in houses, railway trains and offices, find themselves at last face to face with the terrifying fabric of nature. Pasternak's skies are almost palpable. They live and breathe, and their glowing colours are not painted on them.

The world described in these stories has long since passed away in Russia. It was a world where the individual still had a part to play, while remaining deeply involved in society: a world where the virtues of gentleness and responsibility were cultivated; and there were no laws except the laws of the heart's affections. It was a world not far removed from *Anna Karenina*, but sharpened, elucidated, brought into clear focus, singularly unaware of 'the downtrodden masses' and 'class warfare'. His characters are poets, adolescent girls, a woman searching for her lost son, a communist official looking in doubt and horror at a body lying on the floor; and if these characters appear at first sight to be minor ones, it should be observed that they possess as symbols and images a universality which encompasses most of creation. There was no hint of propaganda in these stories. He was dealing with life as it is.

Where Andrey Byely rages, and Alexander Blok groans under the weight of the great images he employed in order to come to terms with the world—Sophia, the Heavenly Wisdom and the Twelve Apostles marching through the snow with the blood-red flag waving in front of them—Pasternak, from the very beginning, was content to watch events as they are. His eye mirrors infallibly the texture of the snow and the fleeting changes of expression on a girl's face as she hurries down a street. He sees the world bathed in the light of divinity, blinding in its brilliance, menacing in its beauty, always desirable and miraculous. They are the stories of a man furiously in love with life.

SIX

The High Malady

In his memoirs the novelist and short-story writer Ivan Bunin speaks of his shock and anger when he heard Alexander Blok reciting his famous poem, 'The Twelve'. He speaks of the violence and uncouthness of the images, the intolerable blasphemy which depicts the Bolshevik Revolution as a divine apotheosis, with twelve hooligans leading the way across the snow-covered plains, and Christ at their head:

> They march with sovereign tread,
> With a hungry cur yapping at their feet,
> And Jesus Christ holds up the blood-red banner,
> White roses on his head.

Reading the poem, Bunin remembered all the crimes committed by the Bolsheviks: the country houses put to flames by the peasants, the engine drivers hurled alive into fire boxes, the deserters murdering at their leisure. In his view 'The Twelve' was more than blasphemy: it was a deliberate and calculated affront at all the values of Western civilization and a paean in praise of anarchy and death. And if the poem about the twelve Bolshevik apostles was bad, the equally famous poem, 'The Scythians', was worse, for in it Blok saluted the coming barbarism, the armed and relentless men determined to destroy everything in their path. As a civilized man, Bunin could only protest against the incoherent brutality of those poems.

Bunin represented to an almost pathological degree the attitude of the *émigrés*. He saw no hope in the Bolshevik experiment, which could lead only to 'damnation and despair'. To him Lenin was an uncultured boor who had deliberately set himself against the established order of cultural values and introduced a new nihilism. He was prepared to accept the possibility that communism, like Islam, was a Christian heresy, with Lenin and

Karl Marx as its Messianic leaders, but this was all the more reason why the heresy should be rooted out.

Bunin's view was not shared by the majority of the Russian intellectuals. With the single exception of the gifted romantic poet Nikolay Gumilyov, who is said to have gone up to the Bolshevik chief of police and announced: 'I am the royalist Gumilyov! Shoot me!' and whose wish for martyrdom was fulfilled, the Russian poets and novelists did not suffer at the hands of the revolutionaries. The attitude of the majority of the intellectuals was one of relief and wonder that the revolution should have come at last, to set free the latent forces of the Russian people after centuries of servitude under the autocracy. While Lenin was still living, they regarded him as a figure of vast and astonishing magnitude. He was the new Moses, the possessor of the new tablets of the law, shining with the light of an almost divine radiance. Whether they were justified is another matter, but it is important to recognize that innumerable Russians regarded the revolution as a kind of apotheosis. It was perfectly possible to believe that God had singularly blessed Russia by giving her the atheist Lenin.

In the early years of the revolution the old culture survived, books continued to be written and printed (though often on terrible paper in the worst possible type), and no one was particularly disturbed by delays caused by the censorship—there had been similar delays under the Tzars, and it was usually possible to get around the censorship by making slight adjustments which pleased the vanity of the censors. Men who had been leaders of Russian thought discussed and wrote about the revolution, employing the old humanistic vocabulary they had inherited from nineteenth-century philosophy; they had no use for the delusively simple formulas invented by the Bolsheviks. They inquired soberly into the meaning of the revolution and its effects on culture, and they sometimes arrived at conclusions which differed fundamentally from Bunin's.

In the summer of 1920 two distinguished philosophers, both in their fifties, both famous and with the greater part of their work behind them, shared a room together in a sanatorium just outside Moscow. They were Mikhail Gershenzon and Vyacheslav Ivanov, whom the philosopher Shestov called

'Vyacheslav the Magnificent'. Gershenzon was the author of a great number of studies of nineteenth-century poets and philosophers, and Ivanov, originally a student of Roman antiquities, combined the roles of poet, critic, philosopher, scholar, novelist and host to innumerable fascinated intellectuals who flocked to his Tuesday *soirées* held in his fashionable penthouse overlooking the Taurid palace. Both Gershenzon and Ivanov had suffered terrible privations during the Civil War, and were slowly recuperating in the sanatorium.

These extraordinary men welcomed the revolution, but for different reasons. Gershenzon welcomed it because it put an end to the mystifications and ambiguities of the last hundred years; 'the naked man on the naked earth' had arrived to accuse the complex and sophisticated civilization of the past. Ivanov answered that such a freedom stolen from oblivion must always be empty, and the way of mankind led away from such mystical simplicities. Gershenzon gloried in the break with the past, while Ivanov denied that there had been any break at all. True, there had been a revolution, the old tablets of the law were broken, but the new tablets were not so very different from the old. Culture is imperishable. When we see the trials and sufferings of our time, we see culture crucified and entombed with a stone rolled over it, but the heart will see it resurrected on the third day. 'Eat my flesh and drink my blood; for my flesh is meat indeed, and my blood is drink indeed.'

So these two men exchanged texts and argued with one another from opposite corners of a bare room, where there was only a single window looking out on some pine trees, and later they wrote down the substance of their conversations in an exchange of twelve letters, later published as *A Correspondence Between Two Corners*. Ivanov stated the cause of culture with noble and emphatic force, proudly and with an air of complete assurance, maintaining his position against the tempting lures of an intransigent nihilism; and though it is one of the commonplaces of literary criticism to praise Ivanov's letters at the expense of Gershenzon's, it is the debate between them that gives significance to the whole.

This debate, of course, has been going on for a very long time. Essentially it is the debate between the Apollonian and Dionysian elements in the human spirit; and like Ivanov, Pasternak was on the side of the angels. 'Let us go away,' says Gershenzon. 'No,' says Ivanov, 'we must stay here, celebrating the cult of the ancestors. There is nothing to be gained by a flight into mysticism and anarchy. We belong here, and here we remain.'

A very similar debate took place between Blok and Pasternak. 'We are the countless millions,' Blok proclaims in 'The Scythians'. 'Dare to fight us. We are Scythians, barbarians of Asia, with slanting greedy eyes.' So Blok affirms the Dionysian tradition, and writing a year later, in 1919, Pasternak replies that the revolution was brought about by a few determined men who have violently changed the whole course of history. Men have changed their nature, have become almost godlike. A great wind has struck the world, but high above us the debate continues:

> We are few. Perhaps only three—
> Men from the Donetz, flaming with hell-fire,
> Beneath a grey and running crust
> Of rain and cloud and soldiers'
> Soviets, verses, furious debates
> Concerning art and transportation.
>
> Once we were men. Now we are
> Epochs, sweeping along caravan trails
> Like tundra to the sighs of the tender
> And the groaning of pistons and rails.
> We wheel together, erupt and touch
> And whirl like the giddy crows.
>
> All over! You'll understand too late!
> The wind hits the heaped straw in the morning—
> In a moment it reaches the roof—
> But in the stormy conference of the trees
> There follows the eternal debate,
> Raging high above the rooftops.

This poem, from *Themes and Variations*, is one to be read carefully and pondered on, for it lies at the heart of Pasternak's attitude toward the revolution. We shall not understand his work unless we realize that he was deliberately setting himself within the humanistic tradition, and attempting with all the strength at his command to resolve the issues raised by the revolution. For him the revolution is the straw scattered in the farmyard by a gust of wind, but 'the eternal debate above the rooftops' continues forever.

'We Are Few' is not a typical poem, although it includes many typical poetic ideas. There is the inevitable reference to railways, the inevitable piling of metaphor on metaphor, the images of machines giving way to images of living things. It is one of the rare poems—there are perhaps twelve or thirteen altogether in Pasternak's work—in which we see the process of crystallization at work. It is a statement of his involvement with the world, but he is not primarily involved in the communist world.

Pasternak's attitude toward communists was complex and unyielding. He was elated by the excitement of the revolution, he sympathized with the aims of the revolutionaries, and in the twenties he was prepared to place his poetry at the service of the revolution, characteristically celebrating the triumphs of the Bolsheviks by writing poems addressed to the revolutionaries of another age. By 1926 or 1927 he was already disenchanted.

In all his life he wrote one, and only one, poem directly connected with communism. It is the longest of all his poems. Largely autobiographical, it describes the early months of the revolution when terror and panic were abroad, and people fell dead in the streets of typhus, when 'the sleep of the earth caught napping was like a child's convulsions, like death, like the grave's stillness'. The familiar images of gardens, trees and wine corks are absent; instead there are gutters, water pipes, tapeworms, the trickle of death in the streets. In this mood he composed a poem which is at once a debate on the nature of poetry—'the high malady that is still called song'—and an evocation of Moscow under Bolshevik rule. The poem concludes with a brilliant evocation of Lenin, not the familiar dog-eared Lenin of the propaganda sheets, but Lenin seen through the eyes of a superbly gifted poet. Confronted by Lenin, Pasternak wrote with a triumphant command of the rhetoric he may have despised, but which he employed with consummate effect.

What is remarkable in the poem is the deliberate elegiac note. Though most of the poem seems to have been written in 1925—it was begun in 1923 and the last revisions were made in 1928—Pasternak seems to be speaking of a time which has vanished in the blood stream of history: he might have been speaking of the Trojan wars, and indeed he introduces the Trojan wars to remind us of the distance separating the poet from the revolution. What is remarkable too is that Pasternak envisages Lenin as the poet, the *vates*, 'the hunter after the last word', the man who can conjure the elements with the gift of words and the command of a magic voice. Lenin appears as a figure out of mythology with power to lift the veils from men's eyes, brutal only as the gods are brutal, but with overwhelming compassion for the human race. In this mythological sense Pasternak was and remained a communist.

'A man must be a witness of his time,' he wrote once, and in 'The High Malady' he showed, as he showed again in *Doctor Zhivago*, that the testimony of the poets is still the most rewarding there is. It is a poem of amazing complexity, but uttered with the full breath, and of all his works it is the one which shows him most completely a man of his time.

THE HIGH MALADY

The moving riddle glitters,
The siege comes, the days pass,
Months and years pass away.
One fine day the pickets tell us
The stronghold has surrendered.
We doubt, believe: the flames are roaring,
The vaults are blown to dust, men search for doorways,
Move in, move out—the days pass,
Months and years pass away,
All the years passing into shadow:
The story of Troy is born.
We doubt, believe: the flames are roaring.
Impatiently we await the coming of the army.
We are grown weak and blind—the days pass
The fortress walls are blown to dust.

I am ashamed, every day more ashamed
That in an age of such shadows
A certain high malady
Is still called song.
Is this a time to demonstrate with noise—
Sounds so perilously assimilated with the earth—
Hurling itself away from books
Onto the points of bayonets?
Hell is paved with good intentions—
It is a well-worn phrase—
They say if your verses are paved with them,
Then all your trespasses will be forgiven:
All this wounds the ear of silence.
Those who returned from the war
Have learned from their ruined days
How the ears of silence are wounded.

During those days there fell on everyone
A lust for rumours. The winter nights
Were not weary of picking up lice,
As horses prick up their ears.
The ears of the silent darkness
Stirred, buried in snow.
And by night we became fairy tales
Restless on the mint gingerbread of pillows.

In spring a shudder seized upon
The upholstery of the theatre boxes.
February was a sodden misery:
Often it would groan and spit
Blood, and then secretly whisper in the ears
Of freight cars about this or that:
The track, the sleepers, the thaw, everything else,
Or how they walked away on foot from the front.

Already you sleep, you wait for death:
To the storyteller—a little grief.
In the slush of thawing goloshes
The lice gather the lie
Entangled in truth,
And does not tire of pricking up its ears.

Although the thistle of dawn
Striving to extend its shadow farthest
Lengthened with the same labour
The long-drawn hours,
Although as of old the road dragged the wheels
Through sands to the narrow pass,
And then bore them on to firmer ground
Toward the well-fenced villages,
Although the vault of autumn as before
Was cloudy and the forest far away,
And the evening damp and thick with haze,
It is still a forgery.

And the sleep of the earth caught napping
Was like a child's convulsions, like death,
Like the grave's stillness,
Like that peculiar immobility
Which haunts a muffled countryside,
Shuddering, and every now and then
Struggling to remember: 'Tell me,
What did I want to say?'

Although as before the ceiling
Is shoring up the apartment,
Dragging the second floor to the third
And hoisting the fifth to the sixth,
So hinting by the regular alternation of layers
That everything in the world is unchanged,
Yet this too is a forgery:
And the water pipes
Suck up the shrill cries of those days
As they climb upward:
And the stench of chop suey and laurel
Cooked in the smoke of newspapers
Defiled the air a mile high, seeming to say:
'Wait a moment, please!
What did we have to eat today?'

So crawling like a hungry tapeworm
From the second floor to the third,
And creeping from the fifth to the sixth,
The stench glorified power and corruption,
And proclaimed that tenderness was illegal.

Yet what could we do? Every sound vanished
Behind the rumble of increasing skies.
This rumble, falling on the railway station,
Disappeared behind the water tower
And was thence borne beyond the forest—
The embankments shone like gashes,
And the snowdrifts rocked up and down
Like pumps, there among the pines.
And the rails grew blind and began to itch
When they barely touched the snowstorm.

So the fool, the hero, the intellectual
Coming from behind in the blaze of legends,
Amid the flaming decrees and slogans,
Afire with the glory of the dark power
Which stealthily like a smile
Mocks him for his exploits,
Or perhaps because
It is not immediately apparent
That twice two is a hundred:
Coming from behind in the blaze of legends
The idealist intellectual
Prints and writes posters
On the beauty of his own sunset.

Muffled in a warm coat the serf
Looks back toward the dimming north:
The snow competes in diligence
With the death which ceases only at dusk.
There like an organ in mirrors of ice
The railway station flashes its riddle,
And does not close its eyes,
But lives on with its misery,
Competing in wild beauty
With the emptiness of Conservatories.

In times of holidays and repairs
The insufferable horror of typhus
Quietly embraces our knees,
And motionless dreams with a shudder
At the spinning songs made
By the crumbling of thrones:

And there comes from the hollow organ
Like dust in the seams
Of the furry shirt of the bellows
The weary song of decay:
And its exacting ear
Still entreats the mist and the ice
And the puddles lying on the floor
To be as silent as possible.

We were this music in the ice:
I speak of my companions
With whom I now intend to leave
The stake: and so I shall!
Here shame can have no place:
I was not born to look three times
In different ways into men's eyes.
More equivocal than any song
Is the stupid word 'enemy'.
I travel. In every world
The high malady travels.
All my life I longed to be like others,
But the age in its beauty
Proves stronger than my whimpering cry,
And wants to be like me.

We were the music of teacups,
Going to drink tea in the darkness
Of voiceless forests, of oblique habits
And secrets which flattered no one.
The forest crackled: the fine weather was
Held in suspense: the jackdaws wheeled:
The ice-cold year stood ashamed at the gates.
We were the music of pure ideas
Which outwardly remained within their frames
Of purest logic, which was
The cold turning into ice
On the rotten stairs of the courtyard.

I attended the Ninth Congress of the Soviets.
In the damp twilight I scampered to twenty places
Before I could get there,
And I cursed life, cursed cobbled roadways,
And on the second day, I remember,

On the very day of the triumph
I strode in bewildered excitement into the theatre
With a pass for the stalls:
I went soberly by sober rails,
And I looked and I saw—
It was as though everything was burning to the ground,
As though nothing would ever rise from those walls.

The Carelian problem shouted from all the posters,[1]
Gazing down, provoking responses from
The sick eyes of birch trees.
On the crossbars of telegraph poles
The snow lay in thick ribbons,
And the wintry day drew to a close
In the contours of branches,
Not only for itself but in reply
To a command. At this very moment
The story of the Congress
Seemed to be the moral of a marvellous painting.

How shall I conclude my fragment?
I remember his voice which pierced
The nape of my neck with flames,
Like the rustle of globe lightning.
The audience rose. Everyone was vainly
Ransacking the far-off table with their eyes:
And then he emerged on the tribune,
Emerged even before he entered the room,
Sliding imperceptibly by, leaving no wake
Through barriers of helping hands and obstacles,
Like the leaping ball of a storm
Flying into a smokeless room.

The thunder of applause
Came as a relief, as the explosion of a cannon
Which cannot not burst: all obstacles falling away.
And he spoke. We remember and honour
The memory of the fallen,
But I speak of their transiency. What was there
In this moment which bound itself forever to him alone?

[1] In 1917 the rights of the Carelian minorities were being hotly discussed by the Bolsheviks. Carelia is famous for its birches.

He was like the thrust of a rapier.
Hunting for the last spoken word.
He drew his sharp line, opening his coat
And putting forth the uppers of his boots.
The words might have been about petrol.
But the curve of his body breathed
With the soaring flight of the bare essential
As it tears through a senseless layer of lies.
And his harsh guttural voice
Which everyone heard too well
Was traced in the blood of history.

He was the face which spoke to them:
When he appealed to the facts,
He knew that when he rinsed their mouths
With the momentum of his voice,
History was pouring through them.
And now, although without familiarity,
And feeling more at ease with her than with anyone else,
He was intimate only with history,
Envious only of the envy of the centuries,
Jealous of their single jealousy.
So he governed the stream of thought
And became—the country.

Those who have ever attempted to translate a great work of
art know they are playing a game doomed to failure. Even the
most dedicated translators fail. Some fail more than others; a
very few have succeeded in performing the wildly improbable
task of creating in their own language a new work of art comparable in its intensity with the original; but no one has ever
created the perfect translation. The history of translation is one
of interminable failure, and the corpses lie all around us.

This rendering of 'The High Malady' fails like all the rest.
The richness, the complexity, the music, are absent. In the
original the poem moves with a majestic pace, with a kind of
slow exaltation and a furious honesty. This is the revolution as
he saw it in Moscow, earthy, smelling of typhus and damp, a
strange crawling monster like one of those ancient formless
dragons which arose out of the Russian forests and crept into the
towns silently at night, without anyone realizing that it had
come; and suddenly the dragon assumed the shape and form of

Lenin, who was larger than life, so large indeed that he assumed the aspect of his country.

In the early twenties there were three major Russian poets— Sergey Essenin, Vladimir Mayakovsky and Boris Pasternak. Only Pasternak described the revolution with poetic insight. Mayakovsky roared and ranted, delivered himself of vast tirades against his enemies, and nearly succeeded in drowning his talent in propaganda. Essenin was a peasant poet who remained close to the earth, improvident with his talent, drunk with visions. His best and most famous poem 'Inonia' is a peasant's enchanted dream of his own magnificence:

> I will sheer the blue firmament
> Like a mangy sheep of its wool,
> I will bite through the Milky Way,
> I will raise my arms to the moon
> And crack it like a nut.
> The body, the body of Christ
> I will spit from my mouth. . . .

Such violent visions breed their own poisons, and soon Essenin was busily engaged in drinking himself to death. He married Isadora Duncan, the dancer, and soon divorced her. He married a grand-niece of Tolstoy, but was no happier with her. Pasternak met him infrequently, and these rare meetings usually ended in violent quarrels. In 1925 Essenin suffered a complete mental collapse, wrote a poem in his own blood, and hanged himself. He was only thirty years old.

Neither Mayakovsky nor Essenin had anything to offer Pasternak, whose roots were deeply embedded in classical Russian tradition, in the severe and almost marmoreal style which derived from Pushkin. Mayakovsky wrote poetry as though the words were discharged from a machine gun. Essenin wrote like an inspired prophet, the brother of Ezekiel, and his poems are deeply coloured with Christian feeling however often he rails against Christ: all the more Christian when he has spat the body of Christ from his mouth.

For Pasternak Christianity was something that had to be absorbed slowly, painfully, over many years and many tribulations. One can trace the influence of the mystical Christianity of Dostoevsky and the visionary dramas of Alexander Blok in the poems which he wrote in the late twenties and early thirties and collected together under the title *The Second Birth*, but the full flower of Pasternak's Christian feeling was only revealed in the poems which form the appendix to *Doctor Zhivago*. Then the floodgates burst open, and he produced some of the greatest Christian poems of our time.

In the twenties Pasternak was still feeling his way. 'The High Malady', 'Lieutenant Schmidt', *The Year Nineteen Five*, showed a full command over his medium, but the freshness of his early poems was absent. He was unhappy in his family life. Meeting his father in Berlin in 1923, he listened to a long lecture on the need for a true artist to avoid marriage, and on returning to Moscow promptly married a young painter, Eugenia Vladimirovna Lurye, whom he had known as a young girl when he was staying with the Baltrushaitis family in the country before the war. She was small and blue-eyed, with brown hair and a beautiful classic profile. He was hopelessly in love with her, dedicated many poems to her, and later travelled through Germany with her. A son, Evgeniy, was born to them the following year. A few years later the marriage broke up, and Pasternak lived alone in an apartment overlooking the Church of the Saviour and the Kremlin wall.

There were, of course, many other reasons why his poetry should reflect the increasing austerities of the time. Lenin was dead, and the excitement of the early revolutionary years had given place to the sterile horror of life under Stalin. A commentary on these grim years was provided by Pasternak after Stalin's death. It took the form of a brief critical analysis of Shakespeare's *King Lear* in an article written on the problems of translation. 'There is the wilful obstinate old man,' he wrote. 'There are the gatherings in the echoing palace hall, shouts, orders and afterward curses and sobs of despair merging with the rolls of thunder and the noises of the wind. . . . The people, huddled in the tent and terrified, speak to one another in whispers.' In an essay on *Macbeth* he wrote: 'So the crimes follow in quick succession—many crimes over a long time—until the forest suddenly moves and sets out on its way and an avenger comes who is not born of woman.'[1]

[1] Boris Pasternak. *I Remember*. New York: Pantheon, 1959, p. 147.

H

Stalin's crimes continued to the end of his days, and no avenger followed him. Not the least of his crimes was that he made the pursuit of the arts almost impossible by insisting that he alone could pass judgment on them. In the eyes of Stalin, Mayakovsky was the supreme poet of the revolution.

Pasternak knew Mayakovsky well, and for a brief period in spite of differences of temperament they were intimate friends. They were complete opposites: the one calm and meditative, the other strident, determined to shock. Mayakovsky wore a brilliant yellow coat, behaved abominably in company, always shouting at the top of his voice and preventing others from speaking. Ivan Bunin described how he was dining with Gorky at an exhibition of Finnish paintings held during the lull between the February and October revolutions in 1917. Mayakovsky suddenly appeared, sat down beside Gorky, gorged himself on the food on Gorky's plate, and suddenly seeing the Russian foreign minister Milyukov in the distance he rushed up to him and shouted obscenities in his ear. The French ambassador intervened, but Mayakovsky continued to bellow like a bull-elephant, while his supporters pounded their feet on the floor and banged their fists on the tables. A Finnish painter who was present wept. 'Too much! Too much!' he murmured through his tears.

Mayakovsky was the poet of 'too much'. He was larger than life, always at full steam, tall and commanding and terribly restless. In *The Safe Conduct*, an autobiography written a year after Mayakovsky's death, Pasternak described the extraordinary impression Mayakovsky produced in 1914:

He straddled a chair like someone straddling the seat of a motor-cycle, he leaned forward, slashed and rapidly swallowed a Wiener Schnitzel, played cards, his eyes always in movement while his head remained perfectly still, and he strolled majestically down the Kuznetsky Boulevard, all the while intoning nasally and in a hollow voice anything of his own or of anyone else which seemed to him profound, as though declaiming from the liturgy. He frowned, he loomed, he drove about and made public appearances; and in the wake of all this, as behind a skater dashing straight forward

at full speed, there always seemed to be some day he had
made particularly his own—the day which had preceded all
other days, the one in which he had acquired that astounding
momentum, giving him the appearance of being wholly
direct and utterly free. And behind this way of holding himself there was something akin to a decision which has been
executed, and the consequences can no longer be averted.
This decision was his genius: his encounter with it so aston-
ished him that it became his constant study, and he gave the
whole of himself to incarnate it without pity or hesitation.

But that iron determination to make himself into a poet was
not the principal element in Mayakovsky's life; there was
another and stronger explanation for his strange behaviour.
Pasternak detected 'a wild shyness beneath his lack of shyness,
and beneath his pretended freedom a phenomenally appre-
hensive lack of freedom, inclining him to causeless melancholy'.
But the melancholy was real, and there was sufficient cause for
it in the incongruities and irreconcilable contradictions of the
Stalinist state. Mayakovsky possessed a pure lyric gift, which
was being slowly suffocated by communism. He also possessed
courage, and his two verse-plays *The Bedbug* and *The Bath
House* were bitter indictments of communism. On the morning
of April 14, 1930, between eleven and twelve o'clock, he shot
himself in his apartment in the Lubyansky Passage, leaving
behind no message except four lines of verse:

> As they say, 'the incident is closed'.
> The love boat is smashed against the daily grind.
> I've settled accounts with life. No need now
> To list our mutual griefs, woes, injuries.

On hearing the news of his friend's death Pasternak hurried
to the apartment. It had been an ominous April with cold
spells and ice on the streets, but the winter was at last coming
to an end. It seemed strange to Pasternak that Mayakovsky
should kill himself at the beginning of spring, but stranger still
was the opaque wall of grief which suddenly descended on the
whole city:

> Between eleven and twelve o'clock the ripples were flowing
> in circles around the shot. The news rocked the telephones,

blanketed faces with pallor, and urged everyone toward the Lubyansky Passage, across the courtyard and into the house, where the staircase was already choked with the tenants and with people from the city, all weeping and pressing close to one another, all staggering and splashed against the wall by the destructive force of events. Y. Chernak and Romadin, who were the first to inform me of the tragedy, came up to me. Zhenia [Pasternak's former wife] was with them. As soon as I saw her, my features trembled convulsively. Weeping, she told me to hurry upstairs, but at that moment the body with the head wrapped in some cloth was being borne down on a stretcher. Everyone hurried downstairs, blocking the doorway, and by the time we emerged from the house, the ambulance was already moving through the gates.

For some reason the body was taken to the apartment occupied by his mistress and her husband. It was not far away, and Pasternak hurried to see his friend for the last time.

He lay on his side, facing the wall, sombre and tall, a sheet drawn up to his chin, his lips parted as if in sleep. Proudly turning away from us all, as he lay there, even in this sleep, he stubbornly strove to free himself and go away. His face recalled the time when he spoke of himself as 'beautiful in his twenty-two years'. Death had carved on his face a mask such as it rarely succeeds in carving on others. It was an expression as of one beginning his life, not ending it. He was pouting, protesting.

Suddenly there was a movement in the hall. Alone, apart from her mother and elder sister, who were already silently giving way to their grief in the crowd, there entered his sister, Olga Vladimirovna. She entered possessively, noisily. Her voice floated into the room before her. Mounting the stairs, she could already be heard addressing someone in a loud voice, evidently her brother. Then she at last came into view, and walking through the crowd as though through a rubbish pit she reached her brother's door, threw up her hands, and stood perfectly still.

'Volodia!' she screamed.

Her voice was so loud that it echoed through the whole house. A moment passed.

'Volodia!' she cried again, still more loudly. 'He doesn't speak! No answer! Volodia! Volodia! How terrible!'

She crumpled. They caught her as she fell, and strove to revive her. She had scarcely recovered when she moved greedily toward the body, and sitting down at its feet, she continued to make demands of him. I burst into tears, as I had long craved to do.

It is an astonishing performance. Pasternak has caught the very accents of the scene so that we are miraculously transported to a spring day in Moscow in 1930. The death of the giant is recorded so perfectly that no other record is needed. Concerning the posthumous honours—his canonization, and the great red and black marble monument erected in his honour—Pasternak was indifferent. Of Mayakovsky's ultimate fate he wrote: 'He was introduced forcibly, like potatoes under Catherine the Great. This was his second death. He had no hand in it.'

Mayakovsky did not kill himself simply because he could no longer tolerate the Stalinist state. Other factors were involved, among them his hopeless infatuation with Lydia Bryk, who amused herself by alternately rejecting and accepting him. That spring she was in London, and he found life without her intolerable, and with her it was perhaps even more intolerable. In his faithless way he was always faithful to her.

Pasternak was no more faithful than Mayakovsky. Women were always crowding around him. Unlike Mayakovsky, who was excessively brutal, Pasternak was kind to his discarded mistresses and kept their friendship. He was incapable of hurting anyone. About this time he fell in love with the wife of Heinrich Neuhaus, a famous pianist and teacher in the Moscow Conservatory of Music. Zinaida Nikolayevna Neuhaus was half Italian, small and dark-haired, with a clever wit and no pretensions to being an artist. He ran off with her, and for a while lived a strange vagabond existence 'without a roof over my head' in Moscow. Of this time he wrote in *The Safe Conduct*: 'In two families, in mine and my friend's, there were

shocks, complications and changes, which were morally distress-
ing to all those who participated in them.' In despair of finding
a lodging, he set out at the invitation of the poet Paolo Yashvili
to the Caucasus, which he had never previously visited. Zinaida
Neuhaus went with him, and they were married a few months
later.

They were months of turmoil, never to be forgotten, for
Pasternak remained a moralist to the end, and tortured himself
with self-accusations. He had been ill in Moscow; the Caucasus
revived him; and many of the poems published in *The Second
Birth* reflect the new lease of life which came with his second
marriage and his explorations in the Caucasus. But sometimes
too there were ominous warnings. All that strange period of his
life is summed up in a poem which curiously combines the
darkest melancholy and the brightest hope:

THE DARKNESS OF DEATH

The darkness of death.
By the side of the pavements
In ditches are bodies
Of the drowned roofs.

Sashes of outhouses,
And the ochre rooms
In a morgue of pools
As wide as rivers.

The cab-drivers lie there
With their painted carts,
And the flaming horses
Of vanished skies.

And raindrops on bushes,
And streets in the clouds,
And the chirping of birds
And buds on the boughs.

They all come together,
They come to me,
Down the desolate highways
Of the Yamskoy field.

While the lamp-posts sleep
In the foreign skies,
The bullfinches' cry
Deafens the dawn.

Once more the earth lies
In silence and meekness,
At her great labours
And offering her gifts.

SEVEN

The Years of the Locust

In those days before the second World War Pasternak was already a legend. With those high cheekbones and melting brown eyes and sonorous voice which sounded like the incantations of a shamanistic emperor, he resembled a poet in his singing robes even when he wore a business suit. Everything about him suggested the poet-priest, the *vates*, the man who has become drunk by drinking the pure waters of the Castalian springs. All the accidental endowments of his physical frame, the darkness of his skin, which derived perhaps from his Sephardic ancestors, his slight limp, his continual gestures, the hands which were finely boned and which he liked to contemplate as though he found something foreign in their sudden appearance before his eyes, even the way he wore his clothes—all these had become legendary. Even in those days people spoke of him with bated breath and with excitement, as one might speak of encountering Shakespeare in the street. It is not often in our civilization that a genuine poet walks in our midst.

Pasternak had become a legend, but he was not an easy legend to live with. His fame was widespread, but very few people had read his books, which appeared in Russian in pathetically small editions. Because he was insanely difficult to translate only a very few attempts were made to translate his works, and those few rarely suggested the brilliance of the originals. Admired, loved, applauded, he was already regarded in Russia as the greatest poet of his time, though his audience remained unbelievably small. His most vocal admirers were the students of Russian literature at Moscow University, who mimeographed his poems and read them in private sessions. They called him 'our poet', believing that he would be remembered when the rest were long since forgotten, and they were continually begging him to give readings, more for the pleasure of seeing him on the platform than for any other reason. He had no magic platform presence. He did not deliver his poems well. He often stumbled over lines, or even forgot them completely. At such moments the students themselves would chant the forgotten lines back to him, to receive from him the tribute of a flashing smile and the familiar words: *Spasibo, dorogiye*— Thank you, dear ones!

By 1935 Pasternak's position in the Russian literary world was that of a strange and powerful adventurer, who obeyed none of the accepted rules of poetry and who held himself apart from all the main currents of thought, rejecting Marxism as he rejected socialist realism, immune from criticism only because his poetry was vastly superior to any of the poetry being written at the time, and therefore he was *hors de concours*. His roots were in the Russia of Pushkin and Gogol. Though his poetry was revolutionary in its techniques, it was founded upon traditional ideas and was overwhelmingly filled with a passionate love for the Russian earth; and all this was recognized by the students, who saw in him more than the poet—they saw the bearer of traditions, the keeper of the Ark of the Covenant.

Pasternak himself was not unaware of his growing fame, and seems to have been genuinely alarmed by it. Rainer Maria Rilke had spoken of a poet's fame as 'the summary of all the misunderstandings which crystallize around a new name'. Pasternak was inclined to agree. He was baffled by it, and sometimes exasperated by it. Moreover he had every reason to know that fame, even poetic fame, was dangerous in Soviet Russia.

During the thirties he was gradually drawing away from all contact with communist policy into a world of his own where the only prizes were those which are won by the spirit and the only landmarks are the fields and the forests in the changing seasons. He was more and more concerned with the private examination of the universe as it unfolded before him. There were no more poems in praise of socialist heroes, no verses in adulation of Stalin or the Five Year Plan. He published little. From time to time there would appear in the literary journals a brief poem or a fragmentary short story; and since he never wrote an unmemorable line and every new poem was a new advance into a territory he had made his own, one which was becoming increasingly familiar to his readers, his progress through this new poetic landscape could be followed closely. And it was becoming quite obvious that Pasternak's landscape was not the landscape of the rulers of the Soviet Union.

What is surprising is that Pasternak survived at all. One after another the writers who had come to prominence in the twenties were struck down in the thirties. They committed suicide or vanished in the concentration camps or were shot by the agents of the secret police. Russia was a police state in the grip of terror, and Stalin was perfectly prepared to sacrifice even famous writers if he felt they were lukewarm to his regime. Pasternak himself said he survived those years 'by a series of miracles, over which I had no control whatsoever'. Many times he was close to suicide. He never learned why he was spared. It is possible that he was spared because Stalin recognized that he possessed precisely those strange and almost superhuman powers which are given only to poets. He would strike down novelists without a qualm. It was not so easy to strike down a great poet.

Though Stalin rarely read poetry, he had a healthy respect for the function of poetry to change men's lives. Like all dictators, he especially feared poems written against himself. One day in 1932, in Pasternak's Moscow apartment, the poet Osip Mandelstam recited some verses he had just composed which ridiculed Stalin. Mandelstam was a small thin nervous man with a bulbous head balanced on a stalk-like neck. He had flaming red hair, and immense moral courage. After he had recited the poem there was a long silence. It was tacitly agreed that the poem was best forgotten, but some days later news of the poem reached Stalin, who ordered the arrest of the offender. Mandelstam's wife appealed to Pasternak, begging him to intervene for the life of her husband. Pasternak did what he could, and he was staying in the country when the telephone bell rang and he was told that someone in Moscow wanted to talk to him. It was Stalin. Thoroughly alarmed because Stalin had tracked him down when he was staying in a friend's *dacha*, Pasternak assumed that it was his turn to go to jail. But Stalin was only interested in Mandelstam. He asked why Pasternak had dared to intervene, and Pasternak answered that he was always interested in the fate of a brother poet, a good poet, a man from whom he had learned a great deal. 'But is he a great poet?' Stalin asked. To this Pasternak replied evasively that greatness in poetry is not something that can be measured, just as one cannot measure the beauty of beautiful women. Stalin repeated the question. Again Pasternak was evasive. 'I want to know whether he is a great poet,' Stalin said emphatically, and this time Pasternak replied that he was indeed a great poet deserving of every protection. Stalin said no more. He had discovered what he wanted to know. Mandelstam was not shot. He was banished to an obscure town in the provinces, and a few years later allowed to return to Moscow. As an incorrigible enemy of the regime he was later exiled to Vladivostok. He died in a Siberian concentration camp in 1940.

In the same year that Mandelstam was exiled, Pasternak had another close brush with Stalin of an even more mysterious character. Early in November Stalin's wife Alliluyeva died mysteriously—it is almost certain that she was shot in the abdomen by Stalin in a drunken rage. Thirty-three established Soviet writers wrote a collective letter of condolence remarkable for its frigidity and vulgarity. Among them were Boris Pilnyak and Mikhail Koltzov, who were eventually to perish in the purges. Pasternak refused to sign it, but instead added a short note indicating that he had read the letter but preferred to make his own statement. He wrote:

> I share the feelings of my comrades. On the evening before, I found myself thinking profoundly and persistently about Stalin for the first time from the point of view of an artist. In the morning I read the news. I was shaken exactly as though I had been present, as though I had lived through it and seen everything.
>
> BORIS PASTERNAK

In this alarming and enigmatical statement, suggesting unsuspected powers of clairvoyance, clearly written under the pressure of great emotion, Pasternak seemed to be emphasizing his own isolation and at the same time indicating his close affinity to Alliluyeva, in whose death he had mysteriously shared. It is certain that Stalin read the statement, and it is almost certain that he was deeply moved and even frightened by Pasternak's implied claim that he was *poetically* present at her death. The danger of arrest, exile or execution hung over him until the day of his own death.

The years between 1930 and 1940 were the most dangerous of all. They were the years when Stalin demanded implicit obedience to all his whims. He ruled like an Oriental despot through the secret police, and smiled pleasantly when the crowds chanted 'Glory to great Stalin'. Every issue of *Pravda* sang his praises, every village had its statue of him. Poets like Alexey Surkov made a career of singing his praises, and Pasternak remained silent.

He had defenders in high places, for there were men of taste and culture in the government; most of them were to be liquidated in the purges. At the first Congress of Soviet Writers held in 1934 Bukharin came to Pasternak's defence with an eloquent appeal in favour of his poetry. Surkov demanded that Pasternak should write about the problems of the Soviet state. Pasternak defended himself as well as he could, a little tortuously, insisting gently that he had not yet 'acquired the right to write like a communist', while holding fast to his own very personal view of poetry. The debate has considerable importance, and the more important passages are quoted here:

NIKOLAY BUKHARIN:

Boris Pasternak is one of those poets who stand remote from the problems of the present time, and this is true even if we give these words their largest possible significance. He is the singer of the old intelligentsia, which in time became the Soviet intelligentsia. No one doubts his acquiescence to the Revolution: nevertheless he holds himself aloof from the dynamics of our time with their strident battles and passionate wars. He has broken with the ancient world, or rather he has been torn out of it by the roots, ever since the time of the imperialist wars; since then he has held himself 'above the battle'. Profoundly despising the bloody struggle, and the conflicts produced by bourgeois capitalism, he has turned his back on them, he

has departed from this world and entered the pearly shell
of his own personal emotions, where with infinite delicacy
and tenderness he continues, with faint shudderings, to
work on the problems of his wounded heart—that heart
which is so easy to wound. Hence this art of the laboratory,
which is so modest, so involved with itself, this stubborn
and painstaking work on the nature of form and of language, deriving its materials from our 'common heritage';
hence also those associations and the weaving together of
the movements of the soul which are so profoundly personal and at the same time so very limited:

> With a muffler round my throat,
> Shielding myself with the palm of my hand,
> I'll shout across the courtyard: 'Dear ones,
> What millennium are you celebrating out there?'
>
> Who cleared that pathway to my door,
> That hole all choked with sleet and snow,
> While I was smoking with Lord Byron
> And drinking wine with Edgar Allan Poe! . . .[1]

We see that Pasternak is completely original, and that is
his strength and his weakness. His strength, because it
removes him at an infinite distance from the banal, from
clichés, from rhymed prose. His weakness, because origi-
nality is transformed in him into egocentricity, when the
images are no longer comprehensible, when the trembling
of his breathless rhythms and the meanderings of his lin-
guistic armoury, though contrived with exquisite precision,
become showers of erratic images which no longer possess
any recognizable meaning, for they arise out of the most
intimate recesses of subjectivity. Yet you will find admirable images in his poetry, as when he speaks of a garden
'sprinkled and speckled with a million blue tears', or when
he speaks in 'The Sultry Night' of the dust 'swallowing up
the rain in pellets'.

He remains one of the most admirable poets of our time,
having given us, by virtue of his creative powers, a great

[1] From 'About These Verses', in *My Sister Life*.

cornucopia of pure lyrics, and he has also given us in *The Year Nineteen Five* and *Lieutenant Schmidt*, revolutionary works of profound authenticity.

ALEXEY SURKOV:

The history of lyric poetry in the world demonstrates that poetic genius always manifests itself as the expression of the most audacious ideas of the time, those which extend farthest in time. That is why it appears to me that the immense talent of Boris Pasternak will never fully reveal itself until he has attached himself fully to the gigantic, powerful and shining forces liberated by the Revolution; and he will become a great poet only when he has organically absorbed the Revolution into himself.

This will come about only when Pasternak, having seduced the whole universe while employing only a very small portion of his talent, decides to move in the opposite direction—into the real world. When this happens, his circle of readers, instead of being the small limited circle it is now, will be counted in the hundreds of thousands.

BORIS PASTERNAK:

Comrades, I have not come of my own will to the platform. I have come because I felt that if I did not appear before you, you would go away with false ideas about me.

For twelve days, sitting among my comrades, I have conducted a long silent conversation with you all. We have been exchanging looks and tears of emotion; we have spoken in sign language and with gifts of flowers. For twelve days we have been united in the overwhelming joy of knowing that poetry is born spontaneously in the language of conversation with the men of today who have freed themselves from the chains of property and who are now swimming and flying into the immense spaces of the humanly possible. . . .

What is poetry, comrades, assuming that poetry exists? Poetry is prose, not in the sense that poetry is the prose work of such-and-such an author, but in the sense of prose in action freed from the necessity of narration. Poetry is organic language: the language of life. So it follows that like everything else in this world, it can be good or bad according to whether we are able to preserve it from distortions or destruction. Poetry is pure prose.

The Party tells us to remain close to the masses. As for myself, I have never acquired the right to speak in the language of the Party. I would say only this—never surrender your personality, and this is a statement which the Party can never reject. The people and the state surround us with their warm affection, and so there is always the danger that we shall be transformed into high literary functionaries. Therefore let us keep our distance, but gently, so that we may remain faithful to the springs of poetry, in the name of our great love for our country and for the men who are its principal adornments, in the name of the love which remains fruitful and full of attachment to the world of reality.

According to the stenographic reports Pasternak's speech was greeted with prolonged applause. The applause was perhaps a tribute to his deftness, for he had most emphatically rejected Surkov's appeal without giving cause for complaint. 'The people and the state surround us with their warm affection' was one of Surkov's favourite clichés, Pasternak turned the cliché against his adversary. Nor was it likely that Pasternak was thinking of Stalin when he spoke of the men who were 'the principal adornments of the country'. But in Soviet Russia even the deftest revolutionaries must pay the penalty. In his autobiography he relates that for the whole of the following year he suffered from insomnia and was on the verge of complete collapse.

He was still in a state of collapse when he attended the first International Congress of Writers in Defence of Culture, which was held in Paris in June 1935. The Congress was designed as a protest against advancing fascism, and became a sounding board for communists and their converts. Only the Soviet delegation was singularly lacking in true communists, for it included Isaac Babel, Nikolay Tikhonov, Ilya Ehrenburg and the improbable Mikhail Koltzov, who kept three mistresses and occupied three administrative posts including the editorship of *Pravda* and who was purged shortly after the failure of his mission to Madrid during the Civil War in Spain. In those days André Malraux was flirting with communism. 'Communism,' he wrote, 'restores fertility to the individual.' It was an opinion shared with some reservations by André Gide, who also attended the Congress. Pasternak, introduced by Malraux from the platform as 'one of the greatest poets of our time', spoke briefly and mysteriously about the nature of the poet's task without ever mentioning communism. He spoke of the grass, of happiness, of the time when all men will be artists. Only fragments of his speech have survived in French, and no Russian journal seems to have troubled to report his words. He said:

> I will speak now of poetry, not of sickness. There will always be poetry in the grass, and it will always be necessary to bend down and receive: and surely grass is altogether too simple to be discussed in assemblies. Poetry will always be an organic function of a happy human being, overflowing with all the felicity of language, trembling in the native heart always heavy with its burdens [*crispée dans le coeur natal toujours lourd de sa charge*], and the more happy men there are in the world, the easier it will be to become an artist.

It was an oracular speech, such as might have been made by some ancient and bearded poet from another age, but it served its purpose of reminding the audience that there were issues more permanent than anti-fascism. Though he attended all the sessions of the Congress, he never spoke again. He was still suffering from insomnia and was not yet free of the haunting menace of a nervous breakdown. Stories were told of his rudeness and abruptness. He refused to lunch with Cocteau and Malraux, explaining that he hated to watch people eat, but it is more likely that he was afraid to discuss the problems of remaining a lyric poet under the Soviets. They were serious problems; he was facing them as well as he could; but there were no solutions.

These problems assumed an acute form when Marina Tsvetaeva, a lyric poet of magnificent accomplishment, then living in Paris, sought him out and asked him whether she should return to Russia. She was bitterly unhappy in Paris, where there was almost no audience for her verses; and she shared with Pasternak an overwhelming passion for the Russian earth. During the Civil War her sympathies were with the Whites: her husband had fought with the White Guards, though later he seems to have become a Soviet secret agent in France. Pasternak warned her of the difficulties she would face, hesitated to offer advice, but continued to correspond with her during the following years. In 1940 Marina Tsvetaeva left France and made her way to Moscow with her family. Her husband was arrested and shot; her son died fighting; her daughter vanished, apparently into prison; and the poetess hanged herself. 'The tragedy of this family,' wrote Pasternak, 'infinitely exceeded all my fears.' Such a tragedy, he knew, could very easily have occurred in his own family.

There was another Congress of Soviet Writers in February 1936. This time it was held at Minsk. Eight months had passed since he addressed the Congress in Paris with his strange discourse on grass; this time there was to be no fumbling. In a long speech he threw caution to the winds and openly attacked the men he regarded as the enemies of poetry, who produced verses on a quota system as though they were Stakhanovites, and always insisted on 'bringing poetry down to the people'. A certain Bezimensky accused him of refusing to travel and to read his poetry to the workers. He answered that he had other things to do. Pushkin had not travelled in this way, but had travelled in his works. Platform victories were trivial and artificial; he had long ago decided to avoid the life of the professional performer, the trained poodle who displays his tricks before a proletarian audience. Mayakovsky had a genius for the platform—he had performed so successfully that he had expiated in advance whole generations of circus performers—but this was no reason to continue the tradition. Pasternak spoke of poems being 'stamped out like machine parts'. And if the poems were bad, the poets criticizing each other were worse, for they criticized with relentless triviality the most trivial of poems.

In his speech at Minsk Pasternak was in fighting trim. Essentially gentle, he rarely gave way to sarcasm, but he showed

I

unsuspecting powers of sarcasm when he declared: 'I do not remember a decree which forbids the exercise of genius: if there were such a decree, some of our leaders would have to punish themselves.' Earlier he said: 'Art is unthinkable without risk and the sacrifice of soul. Our task is to achieve freedom for ourselves and full rein for our imaginations.' These words, which may appear sententious to an English reader, were in fact astonishingly daring in Soviet Russia in 1936; and he was perfectly aware that he was offering hostages to fortune. The most amazing passage of that long speech is a cry of defiance:

> I shall not repeat what you have been saying, comrades, but I shall dispute with you. Since you are in the majority, the dispute will have a fatal issue, and will be in your favour. For myself, I dare not hope, but I have no choice. I am now living this, and cannot do otherwise.

Such boldness was eminently dangerous, but is was perhaps less dangerous than submission to the will of the majority. The stenographic report of the Congress shows that his speech was greeted with 'tumultuous and prolonged applause'.

Meanwhile he was spending more time speaking about poetry than writing it. The flow had stopped, or nearly stopped. He wrote seven short travel pieces in the spring of 1936, none of them distinguished, but that winter he composed four poems on the subject of the artist which are among the greatest things he ever wrote. They are intensely personal; they shout defiance; they proclaim the power and independence of the poet with unmistakable candour. At least one of these poems should be quoted here to show the extraordinary exhilaration which he experienced in that dangerous winter.

There is a sense in which this is the first of the religious poems which culminated in the long series of religious poems at the end of *Doctor Zhivago*. The original inspiration of the poem seems to have been the vast and beautiful wall of mosaics in the eleventh-century monastery of Ghelati on one of the spurs of the Georgian mountains near the Black Sea. There are mosaics of the kings of Georgia, of archangels, of the Virgin, and there too is the jewelled tomb of King David, the founder of the monastery.

THE ARTIST

He appears. Centuries. Ghelati.
Somewhere all the torches blaze,
And columns of marching soldiers are
Led before the judgment seat.

Again the ages. Generations
Pass before his eyes, while he
Whispers into sluggish ears
About his visionary dreams.

I am no faint-hearted man:
But strong for teeth to bite upon.
Time alone will spare my labour
From your carping currycomb.

Are the doors of ages locked?
Are fortresses and temples closed?
I'll spur my horse up to the gates
And rein it sharply at the walls.

I am not a minstrel babbler:
My charger prances in the dust.
I will gaze upon the soldiers
From the highest peaks of fate.

At a touch upon the reins
My horse will lead me far away.
I will brave the desert spaces
Which are clothed in darkness now.

Stormlike, comprehending all
Life and passion, chance and death,
He will enter minds and nations,
And deathless enter their traditions.

Advancing, he will transform nature
Beneath the shouting of the hooves,
Washing clean the tongue-tied mouths,
Raising high the waves of speech.

Cities, roofs, and wandering roads,
And every humble peasant's hut,
Every poplar, every hearth
Will come to know his face.

In this poem Pasternak wears the mantle of Pushkin, and makes the loudest boast that any Russian poet has made. Out of his own agony, not unlike Pushkin's, he is proclaiming the powers of the poet and the coming of the Prophet, leaving the reader in no doubt about the wearer of the prophetical robes. Yet as the poem continues we are made aware that the Prophet belongs to another age, and is perhaps no longer living. That immense imperial figure comes to resemble a fragment of golden mosaic hurled across the centuries.

The flood of Pasternak's poetry had become only a trickle in the thirties. After these four poems written in the winter of 1936, he wrote no more until the German invasion of Russia

They were not propitious times for poets. Gorky died in 1936 in mysterious circumstances; to the last he had defended the autonomy of literature. In high places there was only Bukharin who could speak for the free growth of literature, and his star was falling. Stalin had employed the weapons of terror all through his long reign; in 1936 he sharpened them. During the next two years thousands upon thousands of death warrants passed through his hands.

Among those who were sentenced to death were many of the generals who had fought for the Bolsheviks during the Civil War, including Marshal Mikhail Tukhashevsky. Having killed the generals, Stalin determined to exact the last possible ounce of guilt and retribution from his people, and all over Russia men were forced to sign statements that they approved of the murders. One of these statements was thrust into the hands of Pasternak. He refused to sign it, but escaped punishment because one of his friends forged his signature or because no one pointed out the glaring omission of his signature. There are a number of versions of the story, the fullest being given by the Swedish professor Nils Åke Nilsson, who quoted Pasternak as saying:

On one occasion they came to me with something they wanted me to sign. It was to the effect that I approved of the party's executing the generals. In a sense this was a proof of their confidence in me. They did not go to those who were on the list for liquidation. My wife was pregnant. She cried, and begged me to sign, but I couldn't. That day I examined the pros and cons of my own survival. I was convinced that I would be arrested—my turn had come. I was prepared for it. I abhorred all this blood and I couldn't stand it any longer. But nothing happened. I was told later that my colleagues had saved me—at least indirectly. Quite simply, no one dared to report to the hierarchy that I hadn't signed.[1]

Pasternak was to say later that he spent those years 'like a dead man on furlough'. He had not hoped to survive, and was perfectly prepared to die. There was nothing to live for; the springs of poetry were dry; the country seemed to be at the mercy of forces over which neither men nor God had any control. 'My tongue has been plucked out,' he wrote in one of the poems in the series called *The Artist*. He had little money, but this was the least of his problems; he could always make a bare living by translations. In fact, all through the thirties he was supporting himself with translations. From German he translated Hanns Sachs, Goethe, Schiller, Kleist, the early nineteenth-century revolutionary poet Georg Herwegh, the contemporary communist poet Johannes Becker. From English he translated Shakespeare, Sir Walter Raleigh, Ben Jonson, Swinburne, Keats and Shelley. With the help of his Georgian friend Paolo Yashvili he also translated many Georgian poets. But Yashvili committed suicide in 1937, and in the following year Bukharin, with whom he had been on friendly terms, was executed. He hardly dared to think he would still be alive at the end of the decade.

He spent most of 1940 working on his translation of *Hamlet*, which was published early the following year. He was in a mood of calm despair, and something of that mood is discernible in the translation, which is remarkably faithful to the original, yet curiously transformed. The deliberate raggedness of Shakespeare is absent. Pasternak smooths the verses out, hardens them, gives them an even greater austerity. The drama is being played among the ghostly apparitions of Moscow. In

[1] 'Pasternak: "We Are the Guests of Existence",' by Nils Åke Nilsson. In *The Reporter*, November 27, 1958.

his brief essay 'On Translating Shakespeare' he speaks of Hamlet as 'the judge of his own time, the servant of the future'. The drama is concerned with 'a high destiny, the Prince's life at the service of a heroic task'. For Pasternak Hamlet is the physical embodiment of an overwhelming sense of duty, without any weakness, gentle and violent by turns, always conscious of his rights, a tall man who walks with long strides and regards his courtiers with mocking arrogance. 'He has a habit of staring into the unknown distance whence his father's ghost once summoned him, knowing that the voice may speak again.'

Inevitably Pasternak's Hamlet is coloured with his own emotions. It can hardly be otherwise when a great poet translates a still greater one. In much the same way Rainer Maria Rilke's translations from French, Spanish and Danish reflect his own preoccupations and his own sense of style. Pasternak, however, deliberately refrains from imposing his own style on Shakespeare. Although he always insisted that the translator has the right to speak in his own idiom, rejecting literal accuracy for imaginative accuracy, the translation of *Hamlet* is faithful throughout. There is more of Pasternak in his translation of *Romeo and Juliet*, begun in the following year, the year of the German invasion.

Like millions of other Russians Pasternak greeted the war with a strange sense of relief. The evil nightmare was exchanged for reality, even more evil, but made tolerable because it was tangible. The unimaginable was changed for the imaginable. Even before the German advance, in the early months of the year, there was a small trickle of poetry. They are unlike the dazzling poems in the winter of 1936. They are oddly quiet, reserved, indistinct, as though covered with a light film of frost. They are poems written in honour of the countryside around Peredelkino, once the ancestral estate of his friend Dmitry Samarin, and they attempt no more than to describe the scenery with a kind of detached accuracy.

> When the night enters my house,
> And leans against the entrance hall,
> Then I am filled as with a pitcher
> With water and with lilac.

Night wipes away the crust
From the cooling walls of evening,
And gives that warmth to any country maid
Who is native to the place.

In much the same way he describes the blue shadows 'like ointment' running across a pine copse, the piping of a boy across the snowy wastes, the hissing of the flood waters in spring. He visits Moscow, and emerging from the subway in the silvery evening, he sees 'our descendants crowding to the exits, splashing everything with fresh wild-cherry soap and honey cake'. That consoling vision was not to last long. Soon they were splashing blood, and he was writing poems about the wounded in hospitals and about dead children.

A TERRIBLE STORY

The city will be built again,
And everything will change:
The fear of children roused from sleep—
For this, there's no forgiveness.

There's no forgiveness for the terror
Engraved upon their faces.
The enemy shall pay the price
A hundredfold for all their crimes.

His raging guns will be remembered,
The record of this evil is
Known to all, and what the enemy
Has done, King Herod did before.

A new and better age will come.
When all the witnesses have gone,
The cries of mangled children will be heard
Across the centuries.

The poem, written in the winter of 1941, is not entirely convincing. Almost it is too formal, too perfunctory. 'A war does not merely end in a victory,' he said later. 'So many sacrifices cannot result in nothing.' It was inconceivable to him that the old reign of terror would survive the war, yet he seems to have known that it would survive.

He remained in Moscow throughout the war, with brief absences to join his family which had settled for the duration of the war in a village along the Kama River in the Urals. It was a part of Russia celebrated for its association with Emilyan Pugachov, the leader of the great Cossack rebellion in the eighteenth century. He had lived in that area during the first World War, and there was a kind of irony in returning to it in the second.

In Moscow he was a fire-watcher. One day in 1942 he was standing on the roof of a ten-story building when a block-buster fell nearby. He was thrown off his feet and knocked unconscious. He never forgot the sight of Moscow burning, and the terrible feverish exhilaration which comes during a bombardment.

Strange stories are told of how he lived in those days—alone in a ruined building, in a kind of cubbyhole under a stairway which led only to the sky. From time to time students would come and leave small offerings of food for him. Like the rest of Moscow he starved. By 1943 the German offensive was broken, and he returned to Peredelkino.

That year, after a nine-year silence, he published a slender book of verses called *On Early Trains*. About a third of the poems dated from 1936, the rest were new. The new poems were divided into two cycles, *War Months* and *Peredelkino*. Some of these poems were reprinted in 1945 in another collection called *The Vast Spaces*, which added very little to his fame. The poems are spare. The colour and the dancing light had gone out of them. They are the poems of a man exhausted by the war, who has not yet recovered his strength.

Gradually the strength would return. For years he had been planning to write an immense novel about the events which had unfolded before his eyes. He had made many attempts to write the novel, and had published at intervals some scattered fragments of a work in progress. With the end of the war he began to put his notes in order.

He had survived the terror and the war, and he was to survive the terror that followed the war. Drunk with victory, Stalin amused himself by lopping off the heads of all those who did not offer him the tribute of unreserved acclamation. Pasternak's life was still in danger.

At the Congress of Soviet Writers at Minsk in 1936 he had dared to proclaim his own independence. At a Congress of Communist Writers at Vroslav in 1948 he was once more under attack. He had spent the war years translating Shakespeare. He had written no poems in praise of Stalin or the Red Army. According to Alexander Fadeyev his independence had placed him in a position which made him an enemy of the state. Fadeyev was a man who gloried in his power as Secretary of the Union of Soviet Writers. He could make and break writers at will, and he determined to break Pasternak. He declared:

We all know that Boris Pasternak grew up under the Soviet order, but in his creative work he represents the spirit of individuality, which is profoundly alien to our society. Why then do we fawn upon a man who in the course of so many years has refused to accept our ideology?

I will tell you why. It is because he has never been exposed in his true colours. That is why his verses confuse the young, who regard him as a model poet and as a man surrounded with an eccentric 'halo'. This is the poet who refused to participate in the cruel war in which millions of our people shed their blood. When the war came to an end, Pasternak's contribution was seen to be only a handful of poems, none of them comparable with his best.

I said before that translating Shakespeare is a perfectly laudable task, but anyone who translates Shakespeare in wartime is taking up a definite position. Some writers think that because we hold power, we can tolerate an alien ideology. But I say that we are surrounded by enemies who are attempting to disarm us by inoculating us with the poison of an alien ideology.

In spite of Fadeyev's attacks, Pasternak continued to work on his translations. They were his safeguard, and his bread and butter. His translations from the Hungarian poet Sandor Petöfi appeared in 1948. His translations of Goethe appeared in *Novy Mir* in 1949. He completed his translations of Shakespeare's tragedies; *Antony and Cleopatra*, *Othello*, *Macbeth*, *King Henry IV* and *King Lear* appeared in quick succession. In 1953, the year of Stalin's death, he published Goethe's *Faust Part 1*. When Stalin died, the necessity for translation came to an end.

All through the years Fadeyev, who lived next door to him at Peredelkino, continued to persecute him. It is one of the many ironies associated with *Doctor Zhivago* that while Pasternak was writing it, the zealous hangman of literature was living a stone's throw away. Fadeyev shot himself in 1956, but the danger remained.

EIGHT

Doctor Zhivago

IN the seventies and eighties of the last century a small, prematurely grey man with a huge nose and a bristling beard made a living as a teacher of history and as a librarian in Moscow. He was known as Nikolay Fyodorovich Fydorov, but this name merely served to hide his identity as the illegitimate son of the powerful Prince Gagarin. He wrote voluminously, but only a small group of fervent admirers saw his writings which were passed around in manuscript. He spent his last years as chief librarian of the Rumiantsov Museum. In this sinecure, among the marble statues and old coins and collections of costumes gathered from all over Russia, he spent the happiest years of his life.

This unknown scholar, whose works have never been translated into English, profoundly influenced four generations of Russian writers. Dostoevsky read some of his writings while composing the last chapters of *The Brothers Karamazov*, and these chapters bear the subtle imprint of the scholar's mind. Tolstoy, too, spoke of him with profound admiration, and his novel *Resurrection* betrays the influence of Fyodorov. Gorky described him as 'an extraordinary thinker, little known by reason of his eccentricities'. But Fyodorov's ideas were in fact well known, and both Mayakovsky and Blok fell under his influence. The *émigré* philosophers Berdyaev and Shestov were saturated with this influence, and continually quoted him. Fyodorov's ideas were powerful, because they were peculiarly excessive and peculiarly Russian, and answered to a deep-felt need in the Russian soul.

Quite simply, Fyodorov attacked all the accepted formulas and assumptions by which people live. 'What is freedom?' he asked, and answered: 'Freedom is absolute power over nature. Freedom without absolute power over the natural world is like freeing the serfs without giving them land.' He demanded that men become masters of the earth in an absolute, divine sense. To accomplish this task man must put an end to 'deathly cold and murderous heat, to flood, to droughts, to hungers and sicknesses'; man must utterly destroy 'the power of death over life'. Death must be destroyed, and the dead must be summoned back to enjoy the life which has been arbitrarily taken from them. In Fyodorov's view the supreme task of man was to accomplish the resurrection of the dead, and although he never made clear how this was to be brought about, unless it was by a vast outpouring of love, he insisted that there could be no real freedom unless the dead came to life again.

Fyodorov had conceived an idea of freedom so absolute that it was almost beyond thinking. Yet the origins of this idea can be traced far back in the remote legends of pre-Christian Russia. In embryo the idea had always been there; Fyodorov had merely given it form and substance.

Perhaps because he was three-quarters Jewish, Pasternak was more Russian than the Russians. He had read Fyodorov, studied the ancient myths, seeped himself in the Russian landscape. Like Dostoevsky and Tolstoy he shared the belief in the physical resurrection of the dead. Again and again in the pages of *Doctor Zhivago* we encounter themes and ideas related to death and resurrection. The very name of the doctor is connected with the resurrection. he is 'the living one among the dead', the one who will arise, the dead man who is chosen to be reborn again. In the Russian Bible, the angels greet the women who come to the open tomb with the words: 'Why seek ye the living (*zhivago*) among the dead?'

The theme is announced in the opening paragraph of the novel, at intervals in the body of the work, and in the poem which comes at the conclusion of the novel. He could hardly have emphasized the theme more pointedly.

But though resurrection—a resurrection of a peculiarly Russian kind—is the pervading and all-embracing theme of the novel, constantly reiterated and described under many aspects, most often in the classic context of the rebirth of nature in the spring, other related themes are woven into it. Doctor Zhivago is a man who thirsts for freedom—not the small freedoms of everyday life, but the absolute freedoms which are almost beyond the power of man to conceive. Often he gives the impression of a man standing on a high peak looking down at the small and intricate manoeuvres of men in the plains below. For him the affairs of men have only a very brief importance. In countless ways they have failed to assume the role intended for them. He does not despise them—he is only too well aware of his own imperfections—but he views them from the heights of his own innocence. Like Dostoevsky's Prince Myshkin, to whom he bears a distant resemblance, he is one of those who are 'weighed down with the burden of mystery'. He belongs to the long line of *yurodiviy*, those enchanted fools of God who are to be found in all ages of Russian history, speaking with the tongues of prophets, fearless before kings, insisting always on the truth of the heart's affections. His Christian name Yury hints at the *yurodiviy* just as his surname hints at the author's preoccupation with resurrection.

Western commentators who see *Doctor Zhivago* as a protest against the Soviet state have usually failed to observe that the book is also a protest against all existing states. In 'The High Malady' Pasternak has spoken of Lenin 'tearing through the senseless layer of lies' and breathing 'with the soaring flight of the bare essential'. In the novel he has invented another Lenin, rooted to the earth, simple and human, concerned with a far greater revolution of human values than Lenin ever attempted.

There is a sense in which the whole novel is an exploration of the character of Doctor Zhivago, who was born in 1889 and died at the age of forty in 1929, leaving behind a handful of unpublished poems. Inevitably much of the novel is autobiographical. Pasternak was born only a year after Doctor Zhivago, he wrote poetry, suffered many of the adventures suffered by the doctor, and saw the world from a very similar point of view and shared many of his preoccupations. But there are elements in the portrait which are far removed from Pasternak himself, just as Prince Myshkin contains elements which are far removed from Dostoevsky. Doctor Zhivago is a composite portrait, and though we shall never know exactly the proportions of the different characters who were combined to form the final portrait, we can discern at least four people who left their mark on him. Two of them Pasternak knew well, one he glimpsed only in passing, a fourth was a character in a novel. They were his father, his close friend Dmitry Samarin, Lenin and Prince Dmitry Nekhludov, the hero of *Resurrection*. That Lenin should be among the influences which went to form Doctor Zhivago is one of the many ironies connected with the novel, but it is not the most surprising. In the last days of his life Pasternak wrote that he had three times observed an epiphany, a godlike light shining from a human face. He had seen this light in Samarin and Lenin, and he became aware of it in the person of Prince Nekhludov. In the figure of Doctor Zhivago all three epiphanies were curiously reconciled.

The influence of Pasternak's own father is perhaps the hardest to discern. Leonid Pasternak had indeed studied medicine at the University of Moscow, and had thought seriously of becoming a doctor. The quiet, brooding Zhivago is essentially a father figure, compounded from deeply personal feelings, with the manners of a more ancient culture. Leonid, who died in England in 1945, can be seen only faintly in Zhivago, but he is nevertheless present. It is not difficult to imagine that his death in exile gave rise to Pasternak's overwhelming preoccupation with resurrection. He had not seen his father for more than twenty years, they had corresponded rarely, they belonged to wholly different worlds, but the shock of a father's death is not one which can be easily forgotten.

Many people and many ideas went to form Doctor Zhivago, but as Pasternak describes him in the novel he is rounded and complete, a living, breathing figure who would be easily recognizable if he entered a room. He is one of the supreme creations of Russian fiction, to be placed beside Raskolnikov, Prince Myshkin, Alyosha Karamazov, Pierre Bezukhov, Dmitry Nekhludov and Turgenev's brilliant and erratic Bazarov, the nihilist. Though Pasternak's novel is evidently the work of a poet untrained in the disciplines of novel writing, impatient of all restraints, incapable of keeping his characters in exact focus, and strangely incompetent in his management of many of the episodes in the novel, the figure of the slender red-haired doctor rings true. The doctor is larger than life, just as Alyosha

Karamazov and all the other great heroes of Russian novels are larger than life. He comforts us, because we see ourselves in him, and he menaces us, because he points to a larger life we are incapable of entering. Above all, he possesses a universality which raises him far above the ordinary inventions of novelists. The air blows through his hair and thoughts quicken in his brain; though he never lived, he is more real than the people we meet every day in the street.

'I don't believe in our intelligentsia,' Chekhov wrote. 'I believe in individual people scattered here and there all over Russia—they have strength though they are few.' The doctor is one of those few. What he has to say directly to the world is contained in the forty pages which comprise his diary and his poems. The scattered portions of the diary, included in the chapter called 'Varykino', contain his meditations on Pushkin, on the coming of spring, on the birth of children. In a few brief pages he covers a vast gamut of ideas ranging from the Mother of God to the strange marks left in the snow by lynxes. His restless impatient mind is hot for certainties. He wants the truth behind the rhetoric. Not for him those rapacious and desolate words—'the building of the new world', 'the torch-bearers of mankind'. The common coins of thought have been rubbed smooth with use, and he wants new and freshly minted words, but where will he find them? He finds them in his heart and in his poetry.

He finds them also in the Bible, for the whole novel is permeated with Biblical rhythms, with Biblical images, and with echoes of many Biblical stories, notably the story of Tobias and the Angel. Angelic presences abound. There is the doctor's half brother Evgraf, who emerges at all the critical moments of the doctor's life like an envoy from Heaven, always present when news of shattering importance is announced or when there is what the doctor calls 'a fateful intervention'. Larissa, too, possesses angelic qualities, blessing and healing as she passes through life, untouched by the horrors she witnesses, seeming to walk a few inches above the earth. There is the mysterious Prince Galiliev, who enters the stage briefly, hinting at miraculous victories. There is also the boy Vasya, whose father was killed in the war and who is conscripted by a trick into the

labour corps. His masters are perfectly aware that he is the
victim of an appalling misunderstanding, but there is nothing
they can do:

> Vasya was a charming boy with clearly defined features,
> like the painting of a royal page or an angel of God. He was
> unusually pure and untouched. His favourite occupation was
> sitting on the floor at the feet of his elders, with his head
> thrown back and his hands folded around his knees, while he
> listened to their conversations and arguments. From the play
> of his features, as he restrained himself from a rush of tears
> or choked back a gale of laughter, it was possible to follow
> what they were talking about. The subject of their conver-
> sation was in fact reflected on the face of the impressionable
> boy, as in a mirror.[1]

The sixteen-year-old Vasya seems to have stepped into the
novel from a Botticelli painting with an innocence so disarming
that it has the power almost to bring life to the dead; he is a
mirror of holiness; he blesses by his mere presence. It would
seem that Pasternak intended to develop the character, who
occupies only a very minor role in the novel, as a counterpoise
to Evgraf, whose angelic entrances are accompanied by fire and
brimstone, by sudden terrible alterations in the doctor's circumstances; but he never succeeded in integrating the boy fully
into the text. Vasya is vivid and alive. Evgraf remains mysterious to the end. All we ever know of him is that he is the
doctor's half brother, and has narrow Khirghiz eyes. He is the
angel of life, but he is also the angel of death who presides over
the doctor's funeral and arranges for the publications of his
poems. The doctor himself is as puzzled as we are by the presence of this strange half brother, whom he calls 'my good
genius' and 'the beneficent and secret spring of my life',[2] and
he knows no more than we do about Evgraf's origins.

[1] *Doctor Zhivago*, Chapter 7, Part II. For some reason the last sentence has
been omitted from the English and American translations. There are so
many omissions, and so many errors of translation, that a new translation
has become an urgent necessity.

[2] The American translation says 'the hidden benefactor', which is something else altogether.

How deeply Pasternak had contemplated the Christian mysteries is made clear in the poems at the end of the novel, and
in the meditations put into the mouth of Sima Tuntseva in
the chapter called 'Opposite the House of the Caryatids'. Sima
is on fire with the spirit of revelation. To her it is all transparently clear that men have passed through the cleansing
fires of many civilizations to be brought at last into the fire of
Christ. The patriarch Moses orders the sea to withdraw, and a
whole nation passes over. According to the liturgical text this
miracle is compared with the Virgin Birth, and the coming of
Christ—His passing over into the world—from the virgin
womb. On this simple confrontation between texts from the
Old and New Testaments, Sima Tuntseva constructs an entire
cosmology. The passage should be quoted at some length
because it lies at the very heart of the novel:

> On the one side you have the national leader, the Patriarch
> Moses who separates the waters with a sweep of his magic
> wand, and by his action allows a whole nation to pass over—
> countless numbers, hundreds of thousands of people in vast
> crowds—and when the last man has passed over, the sea
> closes up again and covers and drowns the pursuing Egyp
> tians. The whole picture is in the spirit of antiquity—the
> elements obeying the voice of the magician, great thronging
> multitudes like Roman armies on the march, a people and a
> leader, everything visible, audible and tremendously noisy.
> On the other side you have the Virgin—a very ordinary
> person, and no one would have paid any attention to her in
> the ancient world—and she stealthily, secretly brings forth
> the Child, brings forth life, brings forth the miracle of life,
> the life of all, the Living Body of All, as they were to say
> afterward. The birth of her child, according to the Scribes,
> was a violation of all human laws, since He was born out of
> wedlock, but it also violated the laws of nature. The Virgin
> did not give birth by necessity, but by virtue of a miracle,
> by virtue of inspiration. And if we follow the Gospels we
> see that this same inspiration—by setting the commonplace
> against the singular, the everyday meal against the feast,
> shows the desire to create life against all opposition.

K

What a momentous change has now taken place! How
can a simple human event be judged in the eyes of Heaven
(for in the eyes of Heaven everything must be judged, and
it is in the face of Heaven and in the holy light of its own
uniqueness that everything takes place)—How can this act
be judged when it must be accounted utterly unimportant in
the eyes of antiquity, compared with the migration of a
whole people?

Something changed in the world. Rome was finished. The
might of numbers, the duty imposed by armed force, forcing
a people to live unanimously, marching always in line, this
was abolished. Leaders and nations were relegated to the
past.

They were replaced by a doctrine of individuality and
freedom. Individual human life became the story of God,
filling the vast spaces of the universe. As we hear in one of
the liturgical songs for the Feast of the Annunciation, Adam
wished to become God and failed, and therefore God was
made man, so that Adam should be made God.[1]

We should not be surprised to discover Sima Tuntseva
speaking in the authentic accents of the doctor, who is here
following closely the ideas of his creator. What is surprising is
the deeply religious and unquestioning tone of the passage, and
the implicit logic which sees Stalin as another Moses, another
miracle worker, whose greatest feats are as nothing compared
with the birth of a child. That man is closer to God than the
angels is one of the constant themes of the Eastern Church.
That human life is also divine life is an often-repeated thesis
of the Church Fathers from the time of Gregory of Nyssa. When
Pasternak says that 'individual human life became the story of
God', he is saying as clearly as a man can that *Doctor Zhivago* is
a divine mystery.

Again and again in his poems and in the novel Pasternak
declares the supremacy of man and of the heart's affections over
all the regimentation of dictatorship. 'It is in the face of Heaven
and in the holy light of its own uniqueness that everything takes

[1] *Doctor Zhivago*, Chapter 13, Part 17.

place'; and since for Pasternak no other interpretation of human actions and behaviour was possible, the story of *Doctor Zhivago* inevitably acquires something of the effect of a series of epiphanies. God is continually descending to earth in strange disguises, and the heavens are continually opening out to show the Presence of God. God is in the violent revolutionary explosion which brought the Bolsheviks to power, and He is in the forests and pathways and the air we breathe. For Pasternak history is spiritual war.

There is an extraordinary passage in the novel describing a long Siberian winter, the snow lying heavy on the ground, covering everything in sight including an evergreen thicket, but from the thicket there rises above the snow a glowing branch full of berries like a Burning Bush, forever shining and consuming itself in ecstasy. For Pasternak the berries are as much a part of history as the summary orders of Lenin or the endless train journey undertaken by the doctor. But the victory lies with the Burning Bush.

Though God and the angels are ever present, the doctor himself is touched with mortality. He cannot in the nature of things hope to survive. His task is to celebrate life, and having celebrated it to the utmost, glorying in God's splendour, he dies with the barest possible hope of a resurrection after many ages have passed.

The doctor dies one day in August 1929, while on his way to a new job in a hospital. His years in Moscow have been full of a quiet misery, finding his happiness only in writing his poems. The angelic Vasya deserts him. He hopes to write a great poem on the city of Moscow, but never writes it. He is on a crowded tram going down Nikita Street when he is overcome by a sudden and terrifying feeling of suffocation, and at last by a super-human effort of will he pushes his way through the crowds and hurls himself off the tram. He takes three steps in the open air and falls dead, while the strange Mademoiselle Fleury, an old woman he had known long ago, wearing a lilac dress and a straw hat with cornflowers and daisies, passes by, completely unconcerned. She is death in all its tawdry prinked-up elegance, and she goes her way to freedom.

Mademoiselle Fleury is only too obviously symbolic; so too is the doctor's death. Long ago the poet Alexander Blok had written:

It was not only the bullet of d'Anthès which killed Pushkin. He died from lack of air, and his age died with him. They tell us: 'Here on earth is happiness', but where are peace and freedom? Peace! Freedom! They are indispensable to the poet—the peace and freedom which have been stolen from us. I am not speaking of the ordinary peacefulness of daily life, but of the peace of the soul necessary for creation. I am not speaking only of the freedom to talk and pronounce words, but the freedom to create, 'the hidden freedom'. And so the poet dies because he cannot breathe: life has lost all meaning for him.

But for Doctor Zhivago there was still a second death, a death infinitely prolonged into poetry. This death is described on the last page of the novel:

THE GARDEN OF GETHSEMANE

The turning of the road was lit
With the unconcerned shimmer of the distant stars.
The road led around the Mount of Olives,
And the Kedron River flowed below.

Halfway, a meadow was sloping steeply,
Vanishing into the Milky Way,
And the silvery-grey olives were straining
To walk on the distant air.

Beyond the meadow lay someone's garden plot.
He left the disciples behind the wall, saying:
'My soul is sorrowful unto death.
Tarry ye here, and watch with me.'

Freely he had renounced his powers—
To work miracles, to reign over the world—
As though these powers were granted him on loan.
Now he is mortal, even as we are.

The boundless spaces of the night opened on
Abysses of annihilation and non-being.
The whole universe became a desert,
And only the garden was a living-place.

He peered among the dark abysses,
All void, without beginning or end.
Sweating blood, he prayed to the Father
That the cup of death might pass from him.

He tamed his deathly weariness with prayer,
And left the garden. His disciples
Lay on the earth, drowsy with sleep,
Sprawling amid the wayside grasses.

He awakened them. 'God has granted you
Life in my time, and yet you waste your time.
The hour of the Son of Man has come:
To deliver Himself into the hands of sinners.'

Hardly had he spoken when there came
From somewhere unknown a rabble of slaves and thieves.
Flames, swords, and at their head—Judas
With a traitor's kiss on his lips.

Peter drew his sword, and smote at them,
And cut off a cut-throat's ear.
'No quarrel is resolved by swords,' he heard.
'Put thy sword back again.'

'Could not my Father send a whole army
Of winged legions to defend me?
Not a hair of my head would be touched,
My enemies would scatter without a trace.

'But the book of life has reached a page
Which is the most precious holy page of all.
What has been written must be fulfilled.
Then let it be fulfilled. Amen.

'Know that the passage of centuries is a parable
Which in its passing bursts into flame.
In the name of the terrible Majesty,
I shall go freely to my grave, in agony.

'I shall go to my grave. On the third day
I shall rise again. Like barges floating downriver,
So shall the centuries floating in procession
Come out of the darkness, demanding judgment from me.'

In Russian the poem moves with a grave elegiac music, heavy with dread and relief, with a kind of strange innocence, so that the poem sings to us in very much the same way as the posthumous quartets of Beethoven. Like many of the poems collected at the end of the novel, it breathes the spirit of farewell; it is a long last look at the world, as well as a poem on Gethsemane. It is Pasternak speaking through the lips of Christ, and nothing in the whole poem comes with such a violent shock as the last words, which in the original have a far more mysterious significance than in the English translation. They are short words which come with tremendous force—*Ko mnye na sud*, meaning 'to me for judgment'. But *sud* means more than judgment. It is one of those words which have accumulated a vast range of meanings: it means death, destiny, providence, the laws of God (*sudy Bozhy*). Charged with heavenly ambiguities, *sud* seems to represent all that is ultimate and complete in the economy of God, and when, as in 'The Garden of Gethsemane', the word is given a special emphasis and a special resonance, it comes with a frightening impact, all the more frightening because the mysterious vision of the barges floating downstream prefaces it.

This poem is almost certainly the greatest poem Pasternak ever wrote. It moves on many levels, and speaks with many voices. There is a landscape described in visionary detail, with Christ walking in it, but Pasternak is also present, speaking in his own voice, assuming the mantle of divinity, while confronting the terrible Majesty—the *tremendum maiestatis* of the mystics. In this landscape he moves with extraordinary surefootedness, never at a loss for words or for thoughts as he stands in the fiery radiance of God.

As Pasternak paints the portrait of Doctor Zhivago, we are aware of a man who refuses to come to terms with the world as it is. He is the eternal rebel, the uncompromising warrior against evil, whose abhorrence of the Soviet state was only a small part of his general abhorrence of the way men live their lives. Inevitably his rebellion ends in tragic failure. He is altogether too weak to fight against the powers of evil; all he can do is to suffer them, and to demonstrate in his own life that there is another way to live. It is the way of love.

Since love is a word which has lost nearly all its meaning, Pasternak clothes it in flesh. Love acquires the form and features of Larissa Guishar, the daughter of a widowed Frenchwoman who is first introduced to us when living in a hotel on the Oruzheyny Pereulok, the street where Pasternak himself was born. Though she comes to represent the Russian earth in Doctor Zhivago's eyes, there is no Russian blood in her. She has grey eyes and fair hair, and moves 'softly and soundlessly', and this is all the description we are offered of her. Her beauty is not of this earth. There is something of the angel in her, and like Evgraf she appears only when she is most desperately needed. Quite deliberately Pasternak nearly always introduces her in association with images derived from water, mist, fountains, rushing streams, the rain, the ocean. She is a silent pool or a waterfall falling in torrents, according to her mood. She represents the spirit of freedom in a broken world.

She is, of course, much more and much less than this. She is very real and very human, and for Doctor Zhivago as he gazes with terrified eyes at a world given over to lunacy, she alone makes sense, she alone possesses the power to keep the nightmare at bay. Once, writing to his wife, the doctor describes her as 'a nurse from Moscow, who was born in the Urals'. It is a ludicrous description, but the doctor is perfectly aware how ludicrous it is. 'There are times when love races the sun,' Pasternak wrote in *The Safe Conduct*, and the doctor is always 'racing the sun' when Larissa appears. Her husband Pasha Antipov, the son of a railway foreman who becomes a revolutionary leader, says on the night he commits suicide: 'You could indict the century in her name, out of her mouth.' Though she has been the mistress of many men, she remains pure and unsullied, because she possesses to an extraordinary degree the gift of love and the awareness of life.

There comes a time when Doctor Zhivago has to ask himself what it is that he finds so wonderful about his mistress, and he finds he can only describe her in terms of the vast expanse of the Russian earth, the sounds and colours of the motherland:

A spring evening outside. The air filled with a quiver of sounds. Voices of children playing, dispersed far and wide, as though to show that the whole expanse is alive. And that vast expanse is—Russia, his incomparable and celebrated motherland, whose voices boom triumphantly across the seas, that martyred, headstrong, crack-brained, lunatic country, to be regarded only with reverence, with her eternally splendid and disastrous adventures, which can never be predicted. O, how sweet to be alive! How sweet it is to live in the world, and to love life! O, how often he longed to give thanks to life, for his existence on earth, giving gratitude to life face to face!

And that was exactly what Larissa was. You could not carry on a conversation with life and existence, but she was their representative, their expression. She was the gift of speech and hearing granted at the inarticulate birth of existence.[1]

He loves her with the same passionate love which he devotes to Russia. It is enough to be present in a room with her for him to know that there is light and air, fields, trees, children's voices. When she is absent, the air is weighed down with melancholy and the lights go dim. She is as elemental as the earth and the seas, and she remains a woman with a woman's need for love.

Characteristically, following the classic Russian tradition, Pasternak never describes their love-making. 'Like the word *sex* itself, all the literature about the subject smacks of an unbearable triviality,' he wrote in *The Safe Conduct*. Yet we are left in no doubt of the intensity of their passion for one another. In their gestures, their looks, their conversations, we are made aware of a passion which includes the flesh and wholly transforms it. What Doctor Zhivago himself calls 'the dark, obscure, unrealistic language of love' is made only too explicit, but the symbols he uses are veiled in mystery. There are only a few moments in the novel where we are made aware that the passion is consummated.

In his recent delirium he reproached heaven for its indifference, but the whole breadth of heaven now leaned low

[1] *Doctor Zhivago*, Chapter 13, Part 7.

over his bed, and two large woman's arms, white to the shoulders, were stretched out to him. His eyes went dark with joy, and he sank into the bottomless depths of blessedness like someone falling into a swoon. . . .

Those moments when passion visited their doomed human existence like a breath of eternity were moments of revelation, of continually renewed discoveries about life and about themselves.[1]

That is all, but it is enough. Yet it should not pass unobserved that 'the two large arms, white to the shoulders', the only physical details permitted to enter the scene, are in fact not physical details at all. They are the wings of an angel, and in those wings he is drowned.

We know who Doctor Zhivago is. He is clearly a reflection of Pasternak himself, even more sensitive and desperate perhaps, and perhaps even more human. Pasternak himself never made the long journey by train to Siberia, but he had always wanted to. He had never been captured by the Whites, and he never publicly showed the slightest interest in their battles, which are described in the novel with a curious sense of unreality. Yet in sometimes offering tribute to the Whites he was following an authentic tradition. Mayakovsky painted the Whites as heroes, once describing General Wrangel as kissing the ground and 'blessing the city he loved' when defeat forced him into exile. The thin red-bearded doctor with the furrowed forehead and the air of an absent-minded professor lived within Pasternak and came to birth within him. But who was Larissa?

When asked by visiting correspondents, Pasternak liked to give evasive answers. He said once that she was 'a woman still living, who has been very helpful to me'. It has been suggested that she might have been modelled on Olga Ivinskaya, his literary collaborator, who was sentenced to prison after his death, or else that she was modelled on Larissa Reiner, a dedicated revolutionary, who spent her early years in France and Germany, and became a political commissar on the Czechoslovak front in Siberia, and then a journalist, dying of typhus at the age of thirty-one in 1926. All reports describe her

---

[1] *Doctor Zhivago*, Chapter 13, Part 10.

as a woman possessing extraordinary feminine charm. Paster-nak knew her well, and at the time of her death wrote a poem in her honour. But it is more likely that many women went to make her portrait, and the portrait of Zhenia in 'The Child-hood of Luvers' is a preliminary sketch which was only com-pleted with the chilling words at the end of the novel: 'One day she went out and vanished, leaving no trace, dying somewhere as a nameless number in the concentration camps in the north.'

Doctor Zhivago is an immensely long novel filled with a dazzling display of minutely observed particulars, of many wars, of many loves, of many characters. But the heart of the novel is the story of the doctor and Larissa, the Knight and the Princess, who when the dragon is slain,

> Strain to awaken
> Only to sleep again.

Over their dead bodies, in one of the poems at the end of the novel, Pasternak weaves his spell summoning them to rise again:

> Tightly closed eyelids.
> The heights and the clouds,
> Waters. Fords. Rivers.
> The years and the ages.

For us, who cannot wait for the years and the ages to pass, the doomed lovers rise in the pages of the novel, glowing with life, offering hope in a hopeless world.

NINE

The Last Years

ALL through those last years Pasternak was a being apart. For more than twenty years he had been a legend, and now he was still more of a legend; he had become a part of the landscape, like the golden domes of Moscow or the cherry trees in his own garden. He was the last survivor of the Symbolists, the only man who could claim descent from the long line of great Russian writers of the nineteenth century. To those Russians who were passionately interested in the fate of poetry, he was the representative of Pushkin on earth; and no greater claim could be made for him.

But though his fame had never been greater, he still lived in his chosen obscurity at Peredelkino, taking his daily walk along the country roads, digging in the garden, working mostly at night on his poems and translations, writing with a hard pencil sharpened to a razor edge, filling the drawers with manuscripts. Experience was beginning to mark his face, which remained strangely unmarked until the last years of his life. Most of his life he had looked like an adolescent. Gradually the feminine face began to assume the craggy beauty and extraordinary expressiveness which can be seen on the last photographs. The storm over *Doctor Zhivago* was still far in the distance.

He was a remote figure living quietly in the backwaters when there appeared in the April 1954 issue of the literary magazine *Znamya* (The Flag) a brief announcement of the forthcoming publication of a novel to be called *Doctor Zhivago*, then close to completion. The announcement read:

> The novel will probably be finished in the summer. It deals with the period from 1903 to 1929, and there is an epilogue concerned with the Great Fatherland War.
>
> The hero—Yury Andreyevich Zhivago, doctor, thinker, searcher, with creative and artistic interests, dies in 1929.

He leaves notes and papers, among them verses written in his youth. Some of these verses are presented here: the complete collection will form the last, the concluding chapter of the novel.

There followed on four closely printed pages a selection comprising ten poems from *Doctor Zhivago*. Significantly none of the poems printed in *Znamya* belonged to the great series of predominantly Christian poems which are among the glories of the novel.

In this way, very tentatively, Pasternak announced that he had almost completed a major work, which he described later as 'the most important and the most difficult work I have ever accomplished in my life'.

There are grounds for believing that *Doctor Zhivago* was in fact already finished, in need of only minor revisions, when the announcement appeared in the literary magazine. On internal evidence the greater part of the novel was completed before the death of Stalin in 1953. What remained was the endless frustrating and remorseless search for perfection; every phrase must do its work, every incident must be examined, analysed, placed in its proper context. He was in no hurry to publish the work. He had been working at it since 1945, and he shared Tolstoy's belief that nothing is lost and much is gained by writing a novel over a period of many years. It was not until the summer of 1956 that he finally decided to submit it to the editors of *Novy Mir* (New World) for publication. About the same time a copy of the corrected type-written manuscript was given to an agent of the Italian publisher, Feltrinelli, and sent to Milan. A few more copies, laboriously typed out by students of Moscow University, were also in circulation. *Novy Mir* published a photograph of the distinguished poet, 'whose major novel will shortly be published'. *Doctor Zhivago* was beginning to enjoy the strange underground life which was to be its fate until Feltrinelli launched it upon the world.

Did Pasternak seriously expect the novel to be published in Russia? The question is of some importance, since his motives in writing it are still obscure. Was he writing it for himself? For the Russians? For readers belonging to the Western literary tradition? For the long-dead writers of the past—Pushkin, Lermontov, Chekhov and Blok—for whom he felt so much affectionate sympathy that he sometimes spoke of them as though they were living?

Some clue to the mystery is provided by the first of the poems, supposed to have been written by Doctor Zhivago, included in the short selection published in *Znamya* in 1954. It is one of his greatest poems, and one of his most ominous. The air is heavy with foreboding, as a mysterious traveller rides southward to the Urals through the waterlogged roads until he hears the voice of 'the raging nightingale', which is only too evidently his own voice echoing back from the pine forests, a voice of terror and extraordinary beauty. For whom is the nightingale singing? The poet never answers. He hints; speaks of escape; salutes the song; and the poem is over.

This poem, called 'Rotten Roads in Spring', has a hallucinatory quality. We are made aware of depths beyond the poet's power to plumb them, and of undertones which are intensely personal. There is the sense of someone trembling on the edge of an illumination, and then drawing back at the last moment. The poem is so important that it should be quoted in full, though no translation can suggest the haunting excitement of the original:

> The flames of sunset were dying away
> As the horseman came along the rotten roads,
> Riding to his farmstead in the Urals
> Through the shadowy pinewoods.
>
> The horse's liver was shaking:
> And the streams flowing over the road
> Pursued the horseman and echoed
> The sound of the ringing hooves.
>
> When the horseman dropped his reins
> And slowed his mount to a walk,
> The flood waters came roaring in
> And the crash of thunder was heard.
>
> Someone laughed, someone wept,
> Stone was ground against stone,
> And the trees were uprooted and flung
> Into the furious whirlpools.

Against the blaze of the sky
In the intricate horizon of branches
The raging nightingale sang—
Sang like a scream of alarm bells.

The weeping willow hung her head
Over the hollow graves,
Where the Robber Nightingale long dead
Sang in the seven oak trees.[1]

Against what evil, against what forlorn love
Was this predestined passion meant?
Against whom has the singer aimed
His grapeshot in the darkening woods?

It seemed he would emerge at last,
A spirit of the woods, among escaping prisoners,
To meet the outposts of the partisans
Coming on horse or on foot.

The earth and sky, the forests and the fields
Have heard this rare note sung,
Measured out in doles
Of pain, madness, joy, anguish.

When Pasternak prepared his poems for publication, he
would spend weeks and sometimes months in arranging them;
and there can be little doubt that this poem was placed at the
head of the selection for a deliberate purpose. It was both a
warning and an invitation; in the briefest possible space he was
providing a necessary commentary to the novel. Yet everything about the commentary is mysterious, subtly veiled,
hinting at passions which have died and miraculously come to
birth again, for the setting of the poem goes back to the first
World War, to the days when he was always riding on horse-

---

[1] To the Russian reader familiar with folklore, these lines are filled with
menace. Robber Nightingale was the name assumed by the son of the folk
hero, Odimantiy, who had only to whistle in the seven oak trees to destroy
everyone on earth. In the 'Varykino' chapter of *Doctor Zhivago* Pasternak
quotes the old rhyme:

> Because of the whistling nightingale,
> Because of the wild beast's cry,
> All the speckled grasses rot away,
> All the blue flowers shed their petals,
> All the dark forests bow their heads to the earth,
> And all the people are lying dead.

back in the Urals and the spring floods were mortally dangerous; but in the poem the spring floods are clearly intended to suggest dangers arising from the world. He is himself the nightingale and the spirit of the woods, hoping against hope that his voice will be heard, hoping to make contact with the partisans, those headstrong representatives of a new dispensation. But even if his voice is not heard, he will continue to sing his rare song—a song which is at once a scream of anguish and a cry of exultant joy. He will sing in spite of everything, even if there is no one left alive in the world, even if powers and forces stronger than himself try to prevent him from singing. The poem, written in fear and trembling, on the edge of despair, is also a shout of defiance.

Nowhere else has Pasternak explained so succinctly, with such a wealth of poetic detail, why *Doctor Zhivago* had to be written, why he could no more avoid writing it than he could avoid breathing. There is a passage in *Doctor Zhivago* where the doctor is riding alone and hears a nightingale singing. 'Wake up! Wake up!' the nightingale sang persuasively, and to the doctor it sounded almost like the summons on the eve of Easter Sunday. 'Awake, O my soul, why dost thou slumber?' *Doctor Zhivago* had to be written because Pasternak had awakened.

But while Pasternak himself was wide awake, and a little dazzled by the new world opening out before him, the Soviet legislators of literature were still enjoying their arctic slumber. The death of Stalin was followed by a thaw, permitting the publication of a few books written in a spirit of mild criticism of the Soviet regime, but the thaw lasted only a few months; and when the editorial board of *Novy Mir* received the manuscript, the ice was forming again. The novelist Konstantin Fedin and the playwright Konstantin Simonov were both members of the editorial board; they had praised Pasternak's work in the past, but they were in no mood to praise the new novel. In September they returned the manuscript with a long covering note—there were more than thirty pages of it—attacking the novel with quite extraordinary vehemence. The mildest, and strangest, criticism was that it was 'profoundly anti-democratic'.

The letter from *Novy Mir* should be quoted briefly because it provides the official Soviet commentary on the only profound novel of ideas known to have been written in Soviet Russia since the war. Blindly, with maddening repetition, writing in a style which is a compound of gutter journalism and political polemic, the editors attacked the novel from all conceivable angles. The novel was unjust to the revolution, unfair to the Russian people, inaccurate in its portrayal of events, suggestive only of a wild self-indulgence and a desire to return to the Russia of the Tzars. The choicest barbs were reserved for the figure of Doctor Zhivago himself:

Your heroes, and particularly Doctor Zhivago, spend the years of the Revolution and the Civil War in search of relative well-being and tranquillity of soul, and this amid all the vicissitudes of struggle, amid general devastation and ruin. Physically they are not cowards, and you as the author go to great pains to stress this aspect of their characters even though they have only one goal—to preserve their own lives. This desire to preserve their lives guides them in all their actions, and the knowledge that their lives remain insecure during the tribulations of the Revolution and the Civil War leads them to an ever-increasing resentment. Of course they are not property grabbers, gourmets or sybarites. They do not need comfort for its own sake, but as a means to continue the enjoyment of the spiritual life.

And what is this spiritual life they are always seeking? It is the life they lived in the past, for nothing enters their spiritual life and nothing changes it. They regard the possibility of continuing to live without outside interference as the greatest possible blessing, not only for themselves but for all mankind. Because the revolution steadfastly requires them to take sides, they turn in self-defence from a feeling of alienation from the revolution to a feeling of active hostility toward it. . . .

You have written a novel which is essentially a political sermon, and you have conceived it as a work to be placed freely and unreservedly at the service of certain political concepts, and of course we have had to focus attention on this aspect of it, if only because you yourself have paid so much attention to these ideas.

However painful it is for us, we must call a spade a spade. We find your novel profoundly unjust, and lacking in historical objectivity in its portrayal of the revolution, the Civil War and the years following the revolution. We regard it as a profoundly anti-democratic work, and without benefit to the people. We come to these conclusions in the light of your position as a man attempting to prove that the October Revolution, far from possessing a great significance for mankind, brought only hardship and evil into the world.

Our position is diametrically opposed to yours, and therefore we believe that the publication of your novel in the columns of *Novy Mir* is undesirable.[1]

Pasternak was not altogether surprised by the views expressed by the editors of *Novy Mir*, and he was not particularly disturbed by the letter. There were other magazines and other publishers more sympathetic to his work. He had shown the work to friends, who advised him to omit passages which might offend the Soviet government. Tolstoy had revised his manuscripts at the orders of the censor, omitting disputed passages in the Russian edition while retaining them when they were published abroad. Pasternak would do the same. He had no false pride on the matter. On the walls of his house at Peredelkino were the red chalk drawings made by his father for Tolstoy's *Resurrection*, and some of these drawings, especially those showing the prisoners in chains, were suppressed by the censors. There was therefore a tradition in the Pasternak family of bowing to the censor, since the censor was all-powerful and nothing was to be gained by opposing him.

There followed conferences with the critic Kornely Zelinsky, an old friend and high official in the government publishing houses, and as a result of these conferences a contract for an abridged version was signed with the publishing house of Goslitizdat. It was a perfectly normal contract. The Moscow radio and the literary magazine *Znamya* referred to the forthcoming publication in book form of *Doctor Zhivago*. The book would almost certainly have been published in Russia if, at this

[1] The full text of the letter to Pasternak was printed in *Literaturnaya Gazeta* on October 25, 1958, after Pasternak was awarded the Nobel prize.

L

particular moment, Pasternak had not fallen ill. He spent most of the winter of 1956 in the Kremlin clinic, reserved for eminent politicians, scientists and artists. From his sickbed Pasternak wrote to Feltrinelli, the Italian publisher, urging a six-month delay before the publication of the Italian edition. Feltrinelli answered that he was willing to delay for six months, but the work of translation was already in hand and he intended to publish the book at the end of six months. He had a contract with Pasternak, and intended to keep it.

Too ill to revise the manuscript, Pasternak surrendered the task to Zelinsky, who understood the workings of his mind and was prepared to walk the tightrope between his responsibilities to the government and to his friend. He was still working on these revisions when in the summer of 1957 extracts from the novel began to appear in the Italian magazine *Espresso*. These extracts concentrated on the passages in which Doctor Zhivago comments on the failure of the Bolshevik Revolution and by emphasizing one aspect of the novel at the expense of the rest gave a totally distorted impression of the work. News of the publication of these extracts reached Moscow. Then for the first time people in high places began to realize they had a time bomb on their hands.

Among those most acutely concerned with the forthcoming publication of the manuscript in Italy was Alexey Surkov, long an enemy of Pasternak, a minor poet and secretary of the Union of Writers of the U.S.S.R. Muddleheaded, authoritarian, given to writing verses of a quite extraordinary banality, he had achieved a position of great power over Soviet letters. He decided to prevent the publication of the novel by all the means open to him. There was not, however, very much he could do. Because Pasternak was not the kind of man who could be moved by threats, it was decided to employ friendly persuasion. Zelinsky and a number of other writers were urged to call on him and persuade him to send a telegram to Feltrinelli recalling the manuscript, now scheduled for publication in Italy in September. Pasternak thought the move unwise and felt it would be ineffective, but he sent the telegram.

The Soviet Union had never signed the Berne Convention protecting the copyright of authors. By signing a contract with

Pasternak Feltrinelli had become the owner of the copyright, and he had already arranged the sale of translation rights to foreign publishers. The Italian translation was finished; the editorial board felt sure they had acquired a masterpiece; and Feltrinelli was in no mood to see a masterpiece extinguished by fiat. He suspected quite rightly that Pasternak had sent the telegram under pressure, though Pasternak himself was to say later that the pressure was always friendly and he was never intimidated. Feltrinelli's overwhelming concern was that the masterpiece should be recognized. He felt sure that no great harm would come to the author.

Yet he was soon to become aware that he was entering dangerous territory. Himself a member of the Italian Communist Party—he later resigned from the party—he knew the inner workings of the Communist mentality; he knew, too, that the Italian communists would implicitly obey instructions from Moscow, and they would do everything possible to prevent the publication of the book. The telegram from Pasternak was received in the late summer. Immediately afterward came a rush of supporting telegrams and letters from Surkov and others, and about this time two Italian communist deputies named Alicata and Sanno interviewed Feltrinelli in Milan, and in the strongest language ordered the immediate abandonment of the project.

As usual, the communists overplayed their hand. Feltrinelli came to the conclusion that they were playing an absurd conspiratorial game. He knew *Doctor Zhivago* almost by heart, and he was not prepared to believe that a work of such audacious honesty and beauty deserved to be treated as a criminal libel. When Surkov himself made a special visit to Italy to forbid the publication of the book, Feltrinelli decided that the conspiracy had reached outrageous proportions, and the time had come to put an end to it. Surkov was behaving like the villain of a ludicrous melodrama. He threatened, cajoled, blustered. He hinted that physical harm might come to Pasternak. He appealed to Feltrinelli's communist sympathies. The more he screamed, the more certain Feltrinelli became that the novel possessed qualities that the communists were too blind to see. Surkov went off to Rome and held a press conference, where he declared his disgust with publishers who would so violate the personality of the author.

Feltrinelli delayed a little longer. Vast issues had been raised, and he was still confused by them. The issue was finally decided when an Italian writer passing through Moscow was given a letter by Pasternak addressed to Feltrinelli, urging him to use his own judgment. At last, on November 15, 1957, the Italian edition appeared under the title *Il Dottor Zivago*. The first six thousand copies were immediately sold out, and two further editions were published within the next two weeks.

Surkov raged. Two weeks after the Italian publication, he issued an official statement in *Pravda* bitterly condemning those who attempted to 'canonize' Pasternak. He argued that the work was a slander on the October Revolution, a deliberate distortion of the entire reign of communism in Russia, a crime against the state. He seemed to be determined to exact punishment; and the face that peers up from the accusing pages of *Pravda* is that of a hangman.

Surprisingly, Pasternak was in no great danger. He had survived the terror under Stalin, and to put him to death at this time would have been a prosaic anticlimax. The temper of those days did not demand the murder of a Russian poet. It was the winter of the Hungarian massacres, and the Soviet authorities had more important matters to deal with.

Nor was Pasternak particularly impressed by Surkov's attack on him. Foreign journalists who visited him at Peredelkino that December found him in good health, even jaunty. He expressed no regret that the novel had appeared in Italy, and he blamed the Soviet censors who could have avoided 'all this fiasco' by permitting the book to be published, even in an abridged form. Far from seeing himself as a betrayer of his country, he believed he had served his country well. The journalists, who thought he was in danger of his life, found him smiling, ruddy-faced and unrepentant. He had completely recovered from his illness, and never looked better.

There were, of course, excellent reasons for his calm demeanor. He had no interest in political activity, no understanding of it, and no belief in its validity. He measured Surkov by his poetry, and since Surkov lacked poetical gifts and

Doctor Zhivago was a poetical novel, he was not surprised that there was a failure of understanding. He would have been more surprised if Surkov had praised the novel. When Surkov claimed that Pasternak had slandered the revolution, and failed to distinguish between the March and October revolutions, and in many other ways shown that he belonged to 'the opposite camp', Pasternak would have replied that he simply could not think how a man could be accused of slander for writing a novel so filled with the poetry of those days. He had not written a political treatise; he had written in his heart's blood, celebrating the genius of the Russian people, in a novel they would one day take to their hearts.

Through all the following months he maintained his air of tranquillity. To Gerde Rude, a German journalist who came to visit him shortly after the Italian publication of *Doctor Zhivago*, he spoke of his joy in writing the novel. He explained how after the long years of privation during the war he found he was still remembered; he had a name which was known throughout Russia and abroad, but he felt he had done little to deserve his fame. Suddenly he sprang up from his chair, very tall and straight, very serious, his long narrow face darkening with passion as he said: 'I told myself, you must stand up straight before your own name. It seemed to me I first had to earn the name I had won, not by poetry, but by prose, by something that might well cost more labour, more effort, more time, and whatever else.'

Pasternak went on to say that he was over sixty—he was in fact sixty-seven—and he had lived through many years of war and tribulation. He had the duty to bear witness, not as a politician, but as an artist. A novel had the advantage of speaking on many levels, to many people, about many things. It could reach into their hearts, and it could bear witness to the truth. With an air of immense seriousness he said: 'You have the right to ask me whether I believe what I have written. My answer is yes: I have borne witness as an artist, I have written about the times I have lived through.' He said he was surprised when some communist journalists came to him and discussed the sensation the book had caused—they had not once mentioned the book itself, or what it claimed to represent. They had spoken of the novel as though it were a bullet directed at the Soviet state. He had not fashioned a bullet; he had fashioned a work of art.

That day Pasternak spoke to the young German journalist as though there were no secret police, no censors, no articles in *Pravda* and inflammatory broadcasts accusing him of being a traitor. He disavowed nothing he had written; there was not a single word he wanted changed; but he complained against those who found political implications. 'Everyone is writing about it,' he said, 'but who in fact has read it? What do they quote from it? Always the same passages—three pages, perhaps, out of a book of 700 pages.' He asked why everyone assumed the book was an indictment of Soviet society. He had written no poems in glorification of the cult of Stalin, nor any poems attacking Stalin and his successors. He could not think or write in such categories. Yet already in those early days when the book was fresh off the presses, and all the furore was still to come, he sometimes gave the impression of a man bowing before the storm. Against these ignorant people on both sides of the iron curtain who believed that *Doctor Zhivago* was a political tract, he was defenceless.

He went on working as though there were no storms in the air. He translated a long work from the Polish, he wrote his own poems, and planned another novel. He explained that the novel would be much shorter than *Doctor Zhivago*, lighter in texture, more relaxed, but he was in no hurry to finish it. Occasionally his poems appeared in literary magazines. He even attended official functions in Moscow, and gave readings of his poetry. Once when some Hungarian communists, fresh from putting down the Hungarian revolution, attended one of these meetings because it was known that translations of Hungarian poetry were being read, they were deafened by the roar of applause which greeted the reading of a poem by Pasternak.

'It must have been a very good poem,' one of the Hungarian communists said.

A Russian, who spoke Hungarian, said: 'It was not a good poem, and not even well translated, but Pasternak read it, and so they cheered.'

Many similar stories had been told about Pasternak in the past, and many more were to be told in the future. He was still a legend, and the greatest living Russian poet, even though the Moscow radio called him a traitor.

In September, when the Swedish professor Nils Åke Nilsson went to call on him at Peredelkino, Pasternak was ebullient as ever. He did not give the impression of a man in fear of his life. He talked freely. He laughed at the censors, who had finally decided not to publish the novel even in an abridged version. 'They say it is a poor novel and its publication here would "damage" my reputation as poet. Of course, that's only an excuse.' Once he flared up and spoke angrily about the rulers of Russia. 'There is only one thing they really want,' he said. 'You should hate what you like, and love what you abhor. But this—this is the most difficult of all.' But the bitterness did not last for long, and he was soon talking about remote adventures in the past and how *Doctor Zhivago* came to be written and he hinted that Larissa was modelled on a woman who was still alive and who had helped him on many occasions. He was given to monologues, and he talked brilliantly, glad to have the company of the young journalist.

Asked whether he felt optimistic about the future, he answered that he could see no reason for not being optimistic. No importance should be attached to isolated official action, the new Russia was coming to birth, and nothing on earth would prevent it from growing and ripening. And then very typically he launched into a long discussion of the re-awakening and certain growth of spiritual feeling, and how the world was moving inevitably toward its long-awaited rebirth. He said:

In our age people are moving towards a new attitude towards life. Let me point out one thing. During the nineteenth century it was the bourgeoisie that ruled. Our own literature tells you about this. Mankind sought security in money, land and things. Man's dream of security was heaviness and stability. Today mankind has realized that there is no security in property. This applies not only to Russians. In this era of world wars, in this atomic age, the values have changed.

We have learned that we are the guests of existence, travellers between two stations. We must discover security within ourselves. During our short span of life we must find our own insights into our relationship with the existence in which we participate so briefly. Otherwise, we cannot live! This means, as I see it, a departure from the materialistic view of the nineteenth century. It means a re-awakening of the spiritual world, of our inner life—of religion. I don't mean religion as a dogma or as a church, but as a vital feeling. Do you understand what I mean?[1]

We are the guests of existence. . . . He was like a priest speaking, putting aside the dry dogmas of East and West, reminding the world that everything had changed since the hydrogen bomb hovered over men's heads. A profoundly Russian poet, wearing the mantle of prophecy, was speaking in the same tones as Albert Schweitzer. He had authority for saying these things. He had written *Doctor Zhivago*.

So he spent his days working and going on long tramps through the pinewoods and replying to the hundreds of letters which began to come from Italy and France, where the novel was published in the summer of 1958, all the time retaining his hard-won independence. He was in no mood for compromise. Quietly, determinedly, unconcerned by the gathering storm, he was hammering out a philosophy of tenderness and compassion which challenged not only the Soviet state but all the existing states on earth. Moved by a faith so warm and poetic that it was like an affront to the cold aridities of modern civilization, he was saying that the Kingdom of God might once more take up its habitation in the human heart. The world, which was very old and very weary, took comfort from the poet.

He may have heard the first rumblings of the storm when in September the novel was published simultaneously in England and the United States. A month later the storm broke, and he was very nearly destroyed by it.

[1] 'Pasternak: "We are the Guests of Existence",' by Nils Åke Nilsson. In *The Reporter*, November 27, 1958.

TEN

The Death of a Poet

In the world there is death and foresight. Our ignorance is dear to us, and what we know in advance is terrifying. Every passion is a blind leaping aside from the inevitable as it comes to loom over us. Living beings would have nowhere to exist and reproduce themselves if the passions could no longer leap aside from the familiar road along which time rolls—that familiar time which is the gradual disintegration of the universe.

So in a mood of profound discouragement Pasternak wrote toward the end of his autobiography, *The Safe Conduct.* Nearly thirty years had passed since he wrote those lines, but he was a man who had spent most of his mature years close to death, and as he grew older he saw no reason to change his earlier opinion that life was a tragedy from which men escaped only in their most passionate moments. Sudden death had always been in the air he breathed. He remembered as a child contemplating suicide in his sixth, seventh and eighth years. His career as a poet was festooned with the deaths of the poets he admired, all of them by suicide. Essenin, Mayakovsky, Bagritsky, Maria Tsvetaeva, Paolo Yashvili, all died by the rope or the bullet. He had examined suicide with a jaundiced eye, preferring execution. The suicide 'dies his own nothingness', but the man who is being hanged at least dies his own death.

He thought about death often during those last months of his life. The autobiographical fragment published in English under the title *I Remember*, and written in 1957, contains a long meditation on suicide and gently salutes his dead friends. Against death, against 'the evil flower', he had only one weapon —his poetry. After writing *Doctor Zhivago* he threw himself into poetry as never before. They are not among his best verses—

the best are contained in *My Sister Life*, *Themes and Variations*, and in the tremendous poems which form the epilogue to *Doctor Zhivago*—but they are worthy of him. The fire is banked low. There is a pervading sense of resignation, an absence of sustained emotion, in the verses which were collected together under the title *Kogda Razgulyaetsya*, which can be translated *When the Weather Clears*. The prevailing mood is expressed in the concluding lines of the title poem:

> The winds lie still; earth's colours now return;
> The yellow sunshine spills upon the grass,
> And all the shining green leaves tremble
> Like figures on stained glass.
>
> On painted windows in the churches
> Saints, hermits, monks and emperors
> Adorned with sleepless glittering crowns
> Gaze at eternity.
>
> The whole vast earth, or so it seems,
> Is one Cathedral; and through the windows
> Sometimes it is given me to hear
> The distant choirs.
>
> O world, O earth, mysterious universe,
> Long shall I serve thee, long shall I
> In secret adoration worship thee
> With tears of joy.

There are poems about a girl's footprints vanishing in the snow, about gathering pine mushrooms, about leaning out of a window in the old house on the Oruzheyny Pereulok and noticing that it was still dark at midday under the trees. There are many poems about snow falling. Snow, indeed, has become the poet's accomplice, the one remaining solace in the world. In one of the most remarkable of the last poems he speaks of the whole world under snow assuming the form of closed eyelids, all dying into whiteness. It is the icy world of Mallarmé's swan, and the poet hovers over it without regret. Out of this whiteness, out of the sheet of paper, he will reshape his own world:

AFTER THE SNOWSTORM

After the snowstorm—silence
And the surrounding country hovers
In fields of quietness, while I listen
To children singing by the river.

Perhaps I have been mistaken:
Perhaps I am blind, half out of my wits,
But it seems to me winter is a dead woman
Made of white plaster, hurling down the sky.

From overhead the heavens admire the modelling
Of the dead eyelids set in deep relief:
Snow covers everything—the budding trees,
The courtyard, every shaving.

The icy river, the crossing and the landing stage,
The forest, rails, the rubbish and the ditches,
All these are cast in forms immaculate
With rounded corners, without unevenness.

At night I rise upon my sleepless couch,
And in a moment of illumination
I see the whole world lying on a page,
Contained within the frontiers of a verse.

These stumps resemble sculptured figurines
Like the white bushes on the riverbanks,
And so I build a sea of roofs on paper:
The whole wide world, a city in the snow.

So in the quietness of resignation, writing poems which are
almost bare of emotion, yet coloured by religious feeling, he
waited for the coming storm. He made plans to write a novel
about the revolutionary movement in 1905, but he was in no
mood for novel writing, which requires concentration over a
long period of time. 'It is easier to write poems when you have
no feeling of security,' he said, 'but it is infinitely difficult to
write a novel.'

He continued to live at Peredelkino. Visitors came from
abroad, and were hospitably welcomed. He was a good talker
and liked nothing better than to sit at table with those who
came crowding from abroad. And every day there was a lonely

walk through the forest, past the small cemetery and the Orthodox church with the gilded cupolas and the blue tiles. The
river flowed nearby, and sometimes he would wander down to
the water's edge and take an envelope from his pocket and write
a few lines, while his dog Mishka sat at his feet. It was a calm,
meditative life, which had not changed for twenty years except
for the interval brought about by the war.

He could feel the storm clouds gathering. The French and
Italian editions of *Doctor Zhivago* had caused flurries of appre-
hension among Soviet authorities, but the communists could
take comfort from the bitter attacks against the novel in the
French and Italian newspapers they controlled. When the
novel appeared in Great Britain and the United States in
September 1958, to receive more acclaim than any novel published in twenty years, constantly reprinted and constantly
being used as a propaganda weapon aginst the communists, the
cultural commissars acted. There was very little they could do.
They could make Pasternak's life intolerable, but they could
hardly dare to arrest him. They could attack him vociferously,
but they could not destroy him. They could not threaten his
livelihood, for there were thousands of pounds from royalties
waiting for him in foreign banks. They were quietly preparing
to send him into exile, knowing that this was the fate which he
would regard as the most painful punishment of all, when the
storm broke.

On October 23, 1958, Anders Oesterling, the permanent
secretary of the Swedish Royal Academy, announced that
Pasternak had been awarded the Nobel prize for literature.
That afternoon a telegram was sent to him at Peredelkino, an-
nouncing the award and inviting him to appear in Stockholm
on December 10, to receive the medal and the prize.

Pasternak replied in a telegram written in English: INFINITELY
GRATEFUL TOUCHED PROUD ASTOUNDED CONFUSED. With that
telegram he brought the storm about his head, and for the few
remaining months of his life he was to live in the shadow of the
storm.

The official Soviet reaction was one of undisguised anger.
He was denounced as 'a black sheep in a good flock', 'a pig',
'a snake', 'the running dog of the bourgeois slaves abroad'.

These were the mildest of epithets; the more dangerous accusation was that he was a traitor. *Pravda* attacked him as 'a bitter little bourgeois who has given free rein to his irritated desire for vengeance', and simultaneously attacked the Nobel prize committee. David Zaslavsky called upon Pasternak to refuse the award 'if he had any spark of decency left'. Five days after the award, on October 28, the central committee of the Union of Soviet Writers met in conference and solemnly deprived him of membership:

> According to the unanimous decision of the presidium of the Union of Soviet Writers concerning Boris Pasternak, member of this Union, whose activities are incompatible with those of a Soviet writer,
>
> Inasmuch as he has shown himself morally and politically beneath contempt, and has committed treason against the Soviet people in their work for socialism and peace, the presidium hereby deprives him of membership of the Union and the title of Soviet writer.

It was a long document, written in venom, demonstrably in the style of Surkov, who had fought relentlessly against Pasternak for many years and whose efforts were now crowned with success. At the last moment Surkov had made representations to the Nobel prize committee, indicating that the Soviet government would tolerate an award to Pasternak only if it were combined with an award to Mikhail Sholokhov, the author of *Quiet Flows the Don*. The committee rejected his advice. Surkov was exacting a vengeance which in his eyes was long overdue.

In communist Russia the processes of vengeance against state criminals are complex, discreet, curiously abstract. The sinner must be made to admit his guilt, not once but many times. He may, like Bukharin in his famous trial in 1938, defend himself, but only on condition that his defence includes an assumption of guilt from the beginning. He may question his own motives, and show them in the most favourable light, but he may not question the wisdom of his superiors.

Pasternak was not an innocent spectator of his own actions. He had permitted the publication of *Doctor Zhivago* abroad, and he knew the penalty would have to be paid. He knew that in the eyes of the Soviet authorities he must make restitution by self-abasement. He telegraphed to the Nobel prize committee a statement rejecting the award 'because of the significance attached to the reward in the society I am living in', and then turned his attention to the complicated rites of absolution.

The storm in Russia was increasing in fury. From every side he was being attacked with concentrated malice. Workers who had never read a line of poetry, and never heard his name, were interviewed, and their criticisms against 'this traitor in our midst, who has fouled the earth he stands on', were printed in the columns of *Pravda*. The editor of *Komsomol* launched a particularly vicious attack on him and urged him to leave the country before an aroused populace took the law in its own hands. Pasternak appears to have regarded this attack as the signal for the first act in the inevitable drama of self-accusation. On the following day, October 31, he wrote to Nikita Khrushchev, the chairman of the Council of Ministers of the U.S.S.R.

ESTEEMED NIKITA SERGEYEVICH,

It has been made known to me through Comrade Semitchastny that the government will raise no objection if I leave the U.S.S.R. For me this is impossible.

I am tied to Russia by my birth, my life, and my work. I cannot conceive of separation from my country or of living abroad. Whatever my mistakes and aberrations, it never occurred to me that I would become the centre of the political storm which has congregated about my name in the West. For this reason I have made known to the Royal Academy of Sweden that I voluntarily renounce the Nobel prize.

To cross the frontiers of my country would be for me a sentence of death, and that is why I beg you not to take these extreme measures against me. With my hand on my heart I can say that I have been of some service to Soviet literature, and I may still be of some service in the future.

BORIS PASTERNAK

Pasternak must have known that a cursory recognition of 'my mistakes and aberrations' would be insufficient. More, much more, would be demanded of him before the attacks were called off. On November 1, eight hundred Soviet writers demanded that he be deprived of Soviet citizenship, and *Literaturnaya Gazeta* published a long column of interviews with people who claimed that *Doctor Zhivago* was an act of provocation against the Soviet State, and Pasternak himself should be stamped out like an insect. Most of the interviews seem to have been written in the newspaper office.

On November 2, Pasternak's letter was published in *Pravda* with the comment that, if he wished, he could attend the prize-giving ceremony in Stockholm and enjoy 'the delights of the capitalist paradise'. It was hinted that if he left Russia, he would not be allowed to return. The time had come for a renewed act of self-accusation. On November 5 he wrote a *mea culpa*, which was published the next day in *Pravda*:

I accepted the award of the Nobel prize as a literary distinction. I rejoiced at it, and so expressed myself in a telegram addressed to the Secretary of the Swedish Academy. But I was wrong.

My mistakes however arose from understandable causes. Some five years ago, long before my novel came into existence, I knew I had already been nominated as a candidate for the award.

A week later, when I realized the scope of the political campaign which has formed around my novel, it occurred to me that the award was a political measure which has brought monstrous consequences in its train. On my own initiative, without compulsion from anyone, I sent in my voluntary renunciation of the award.

In my letter to Nikita Sergeyevich Khrushchev I declared that I am tied to Russia by my birth, my life and my work, and that it was unthinkable to me to leave and go into exile abroad. When I wrote this letter, I was not thinking only of my ties to the earth and to nature, but also of Russia's people, her past and her glorious present and future.

Nevertheless, it is my own fault that my novel has come

like a barrier between myself and the people, although I never had the least desire to harm either the State or my countrymen. The editors of *Novy Mir* warned me that the novel would be understood by readers as a work directed against the October Revolution and the founding of the Soviet state. I did not realize this, and now I regret it.

Indeed, if one were to accept the conclusions which arise from the critical analysis of the novel, it would seem that I have maintained the following erroneous statements:

I appear to have insisted that no revolution can be historically justified, and that the October Revolution is a purely illegitimate phenomenon, which brought misery upon Russia and produced the downfall of the old Russian intelligentsia. But it is clear to me that I am far from subscribing to statements of this kind, which are illogical and absurd. Yet my work, which received the Nobel prize, gave cause for these regrettable interpretations, and this is the reason why I finally renounced the prize.

If the Italian editor had stopped publication of the novel when I advised him—the book was published in other countries without my authority—I would perhaps have been able to correct it, at least in part. But the book has been printed, and it is too late to discuss this.

During this stormy week I have not been persecuted. My life has not been endangered, nor has my freedom been imperilled. I want to stress once again that all my actions have been entirely voluntary. People who know me are aware that nothing on earth can make me act against the dictates of my conscience or my convictions. And in the present case this is still true.

It is scarcely necessary for me to add that no one has extorted this statement from me. I am writing this of my own free will, with a bright faith in the future of all concerned and my own future, being proud of the age I live in and of the people who surround me. I firmly believe I shall find the strength to redeem my good name and restore the confidence of my comrades.

The letter to *Pravda* deserves to be quoted at length because it shows Pasternak performing the classic act of recantation. There are minor interpolations which seem to have been inserted by another hand, but the fivefold confession of error is clearly Pasternak's own. When he spoke of the award as 'a political measure which has brought monstrous consequences in its train', he was speaking the language of his masters, knowing the statement to be untrue. Nor had he 'sent in my voluntary renunciation of the award' without compulsion from anyone. In their desire to exact the utmost penalty, they had forced him to tell lies. It was perhaps the most terrible part of the punishment.

Although he made his recantation, the ferocious attacks on him continued. All though November he was attacked in newspapers, and workmen in remote regions of Russia were summoned to attend meetings in which his name was held up in obloquy. That year the Nobel prize for science was awarded to three Soviet physicists; and through the columns of *Pravda* the Soviet government approved the awards and paid tribute to the wisdom of the Nobel prize committee in granting them. On the day the Soviet physicists reached Stockholm, the novelist Leonid Sobolev chose to launch a peculiarly vigorous attack against Pasternak, charging him with 'giving ammunition to the agents of the cold war' and describing him as 'the rightful heir of the decadent movement condemned by Lenin and Chekhov'. It was an unhappy conjunction of names, for of all men living Pasternak resembled Chekhov most. On the previous day there had been a barrage of insults from *Pravda*, and once more the dangerous word 'traitor' was hurled at him. The pattern was emerging. It was not enough that he make his recantation. He must continue to make them, day after day, week after week, until he had purged himself of his guilt.

The deadly game of recantations was not one which Pasternak could play with enthusiasm. He had made his final submission to *Pravda*, and made no more. Outwardly, he behaved as he had always behaved, gentle and courteous to all those who came to his doors. Vast sums of money—his royalties soon amounted to nearly £400,000—were accumulating for him abroad. He had no interest in the money, spoke sometimes

M

of assigning it to his relatives living abroad, but apparently signed no documents apportioning it. Expelled from the Union of Soviet Writers, which owned his *dacha* at Peredelkino and could remove him at the stroke of a pen, he was living in a kind of no man's land. He was like a stateless citizen, without rights, with no source of income, a pariah in his own land. His fellow writers left him severely alone, and the State did not encourage foreigners to visit him.

In those days, when the storm had passed overhead and only its rumblings could be heard, he seemed to view the world with a kind of amused tolerance, resigned to his fate. 'I am a white cormorant,' he said once. 'As everyone knows, there are only black cormorants.' Gradually he was discovering the laws by which white cormorants live.

Strangely, in those last months of his life he seemed to lose interest in his fame as a poet. It had become an irrelevance. In many letters he explained that he wanted to be known by *Doctor Zhivago* and by the brief autobiographical fragment he wrote in 1957, after recovering from an illness. He consigned everything written before 1940 to perdition. He complained that his former style was 'impure', too flamboyant, out of touch with reality; and he refused to talk about his early poetry, saying he would be happier if it all vanished. There is nothing particularly disturbing about such an attitude, for poets frequently come to dislike their best verses. On his deathbed Virgil asked that the whole of his unfinished epic, *The Aeneid*, be burned, and only the intervention of the Emperor Augustus caused it to be preserved. Pasternak's opinions on his own work are not important.

Once more he found comfort in translations. He began to translate a long Polish epic, but apparently abandoned it after translating about a thousand lines. His verses remained unpublished, but his translation of Schiller's verse-play *Maria Stuart* was still being performed, notably in Moscow, where his name appeared on the programme in small but perfectly legible type. It was clear that the man who had been officially condemned as a traitor still had a following, and could still command an audience.

The attacks, however, had shaken him. Those who saw him

before and after the Nobel prize observed a change in his manner. Before, he was a man looking forward to the combat; afterwards, he looked hurt and dazed, not quite so sure of himself. 'I still want to write about love and life in Russia and on earth,' he told one visitor, but there was little conviction in his voice. He needed a long period of rest, but there was no rest. Thousands of letters were sent to him, and he answered most of them, even the most foolish ones. A woman wrote from Long Island, inviting him to add his name to a chain letter, and he sent her inexplicably a gentle reply, chiding her for her folly, and then apologizing. Young people who wrote to him were surprised to receive answers covering three or four pages. These letters were his means of communicating with the world. The Soviet authorities put no limit to the number of letters he sent or received. They had other ways of making their influence felt.

In the late autumn of 1958 he was ill, and for some weeks refused to see visitors. When he recovered, he looked more craggy than ever, the skin drawn tight over the cheekbones, the fine face filled with an interior light. He was dying, and knew it. In February 1959, he wrote a short poem called 'The Nobel Prize':

> I am like a beast caught in a pen.
> Somewhere there are people enjoying freedom and light,
> But the furious chase continually closes in,
> And I cannot break out.
>
> A dark forest lies beside a pool,
> And I am the stump of an uprooted fir tree:
> All my ways of escape are cut off.
> Whatever my fate, I shall accept it.
>
> But what wicked things have I done?
> Am I a murderer or a thief?
> I who forced the whole world to shed tears
> Over the beauty of my land!
>
> Now as I incline toward my grave,
> I believe the time is soon coming
> When the spirit of good will prevail
> Over wickedness and infamy.

It was almost his final salute to the world, full of his characteristic imagery and spoken so simply that it seems to have been composed in a single breath, without effort.

The fire was burning low. He did little work during the last months. He still wrote innumerable letters, still went for daily walks, still swept out his bare upstairs room with the varnished wooden floor boards, the double windows, the bed and the table where he worked with a view looking over the pinewoods. He coughed a lot during his last winter, but it was only in the early spring that he began to complain of pains in his chest. He complained, too, of breathlessness, and there were dizzy spells, which he put down to the excitement of the battle over *Doctor Zhivago*. He looked in good health, ruddy, handsome, his hair almost completely white, which somehow gave him a younger appearance, and he walked with the same springy step. When the pains grew worse, he confessed to a friend that he thought he had lung cancer, and begged no one to tell his wife Zinaida. Meanwhile he refused to see a doctor, remembering his experiences when he was taken to the Kremlin clinic and the air of officialdom and authority hung over him.

The truth was that he hated doctors, and feared them, and always regarded them with the same distaste as he regarded the Soviet system. The weakest parts of *Doctor Zhivago* are those describing the doctor practising medicine. Pasternak's work is full of ironies, and one of the greatest of all is to be found in his attitude to the medical profession, which he privately detested, while exalting it in the novel.

He was always raging against doctors. Not long after leaving the Kremlin clinic he complained to a friend: 'They sent a woman doctor disguised as a nurse to stay under my roof. I was always surrounded by doctors. What are they frightened of? Are they afraid I will commit suicide?' More melodramatically he told another friend: 'I have never been in better health. If you ever hear I am suffering from a malignant disease, you may be sure they have sent doctors to kill me.'

In the spring of 1960, without knowing it, he was in desperate need of doctors. There were black-outs, but he pretended they were due to strain or overwork, and refused to let doctors come to the house. After an unusually severe black-out in May, the doctors were finally summoned. They diagnosed a heart attack. They were wrong. As Pasternak had long suspected, he was suffering from lung cancer. It spread through both lungs, into his heart, and into his stomach. Dr. Nikolay Petrov, the famous cancer specialist from the Kremlin clinic, made the final diagnosis, but the time had passed when anything could be done to save his life. He died quietly, without struggle, in an oxygen tent, and his last words were addressed to his wife.

At the funeral on June 2, there were no government officials, no representatives of the Soviet Union of Writers. But students and peasants came to view the body, and Sviatoslav Richter, the pupil of Heinrich Neuhaus and perhaps the greatest living performer of Chopin, played Chopin's 'Marche Funèbre' and Beethoven's funeral march on the small upright piano on which Pasternak had played so often. The mourners wound through the house carpeted with pine branches, and walked out again to stand in the afternoon sunlight. Originally, the coffin was to be taken to the cemetery by car, but the students carried it on their shoulders to the village churchyard half a mile away.

No priests attended the ceremony. A few, a very few, writers were present. There were long-time friends like Kornei Chukovsky and Konstantin Paustovsky, both of them approaching eighty, and therefore with little to fear from the Soviet government. There were the short-story writer Venyamin Kaverin and the philosopher Valentin Asmos, and no others. Asmos made the farewell speech, saying: 'As long as Russian poetry lives, Boris Leonidovich Pasternak will stand among the greatest. His disagreement with the present time was not with the state: he wanted a society of a higher order altogether. His mistake was that he followed the way of Tolstoy, and refused to believe in the need of violent resistance to evil. Farewell, Boris Leonidovich, we all thank you. We owe you a large and unpaid debt.'

There were many around the open coffin who spoke of their gratitude. A workman shouted: 'It was a great book he wrote. A pity they would not let us read it!' A young student stepped forward and said: 'Over a poet's grave his verses should be spoken', and there was complete silence while he recited the

poem which stands at the head of the poems in the epilogue to
Doctor Zhivago:

> The shouting now is over. I make my entrance
> Upon the stage, and lean against the archway,
> Straining to hear the far-off echoing voices,
> Announcing what shall happen in my time.
>
> The darkness of the night transfixes me
> Along the sights of a million opera glasses—
> Abba, Father, may it be granted to me
> To let the cup pass from my hands.
>
> Though I adore thy solemn purposes
> And gladly would I take a player's part,
> Yet now another play is being acted:
> Spare me now, and let me go my way.
>
> The order of the acts is well conceived,
> And the final curtain unescapable:
> I, alone, all drowned among the Pharisees.
> To live one's life is not to cross a field.

Then for the last time the peasant women kissed the thin,
narrow, almost unrecognizable face among the heaped flowers,
and the coffin was sealed and lowered into the grave, not far
from the Church of the Transfiguration. Soon there were only
a few people in the cemetery, and the taxis were making their
way back to Moscow.

Pasternak was dead, and more alive than ever. He had become a legend. He was one of those rare men who assume great
spiritual tasks, and carry them out to a conclusion. He had
achieved the truth of himself and defied the most menacing
dictatorship on earth single-handed, and as much as it can be
fought on any human and intellectual levels, he had fought it to
a standstill. There is a sense in which his whole life was a pre-
paration for *Doctor Zhivago*, but he was himself greater than the
thin red-haired doctor who wandered through the only novel of
our time which can be compared with the great novels of
Russia's classic age. He wrote in one of his last poems: 'It is not
for you to retreat a single inch. You must be alive, alive, only
alive to the very end.'

He had been alive to the very end, and that was his glory.

Select Bibliography

Akhmatova, Anna. *Stikhotvoreniya.* Moscow: Gos. Izdat., 1958.

Blok, Alexander. *Sobraniye Sochinenii.* Leningrad: Izdat. Pisatelei, 1932–6.

Bowra, C. M. *The Creative Experiment.* London: Macmillan, 1949.

Fyodorov, Nikolay. *Philosophiya obshchavo dela.* Harbin: 1928.

Pasternak, Boris. *Doctor Zhivago.* London: Collins, 1958.

    I Remember: Sketch for an Autobiography. New York: Pantheon, 1959.

    Na Rannikh Poezdakh. Moscow: Sov. Pisat., 1943.

    Okhrannaya Gramota. Leningrad: Izdat. Pisatelei, 1931.

    Poemi. Moscow: Sov. Lit., 1933.

    Rasskazi. Moscow: Krug, 1925.

    Sestra moya zhizn. Berlin: Izdat. Crzhebina, 1923.

    Collected Prose Works, translated by Beatrice Scott and Robert Payne. London: Lindsay Drummond, 1945.

    Vtoroe Rozhdeniye. Moscow: Sov. Pisat., 1934.

    Zemnoi Prostor. Moscow: Sov. Pisat., 1945.

Svyatopolk-Mirsky, Prince D. S. *Modern Russian Literature.* Oxford University Press, 1925.

Index